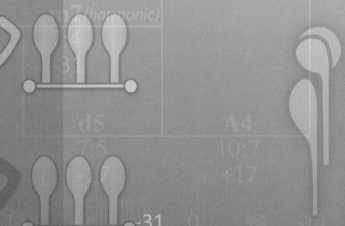

# TUNING FOR WIND INSTRUMENTS

## A Roadmap to Successful Intonation

### SHELLEY JAGOW

Published by
Meredith Music Publications
a division of G.W. Music, Inc.
4899 Lerch Creek Ct., Galesville, MD 20765
http://www.meredithmusic.com

Illustrations: Shelley Jagow
Cover and text design: Shawn Girsberger

International Standard Book Number: 978-1-57463-209-5
Cataloging-in-Publication Data is on file with the Library of Congress.
Library of Congress Control Number: 2012948453
Printed and bound in U.S.A.

21  20  19  18  17  PP  6  7  8  9  10

# Contents

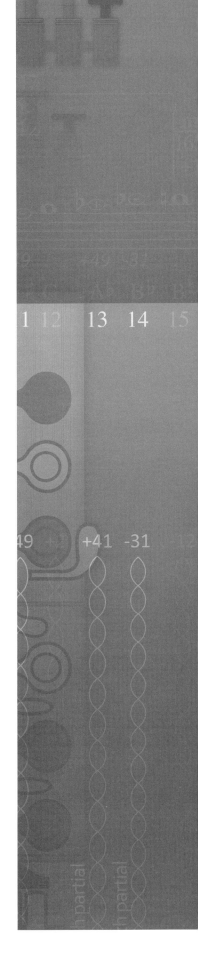

# List of Figures

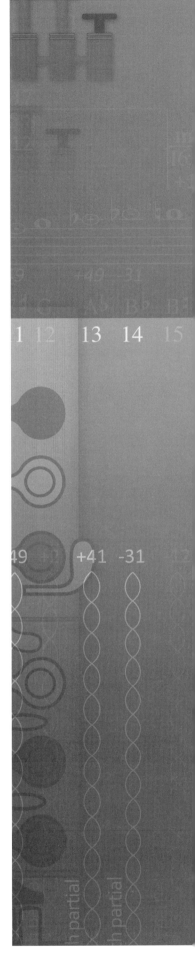

# List of Tables

# Acknowledgement

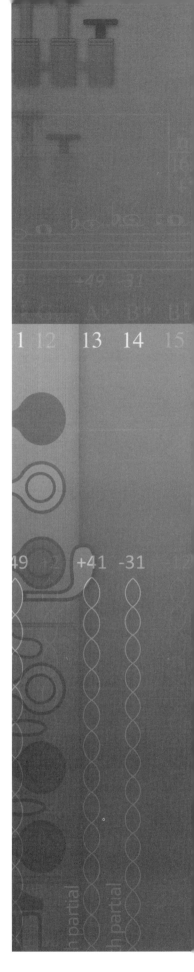

Without the support and encouragement from family, friends, students and colleagues, this resource would never have blossomed to the labor of love that it now carries. First and foremost, I would like to thank Kimberly Carr for the hundreds upon hundreds of hours she patiently endured as I borrowed our time to research and write this book, and spend countless hours designing the graphics for the fingering charts from scratch. As with my first book, Kim was there to extinguish doubt with faith, to replace fatigue with energy, and to fuel my creativity when the tank was near empty. Thank you Kim for being you! I am also thankful for my students for their continued assurance and support. I feel privileged to work at a University that inspires innovation, models extraordinary leadership, and attracts young music educators that inspire and motivate me daily. I am also very grateful to the many colleagues across North America who gave of their time to provide feedback on the fingering charts for each instrument. Although difficult to reach a 100 percent consensus of opinion, your thorough reviews assisted in providing the most current and practical intonation charts for ensemble players.

# Introduction

We all seek the intonation holy grail in pursuit of answering all our ensemble pitch problems. Unfortunately, no such grail exists because the factors that affect pitch are too abundant and the pros and cons for the various tuning systems are many and varied.

The area of intonation can invoke challenges and apprehension in the classroom for both student and teacher. This book will assist in clarifying some of the mystical issues of intonation and provide not only techniques for teaching intonation, but also provide charts for every common wind band instrument with suggested fingerings for improving intonation. Foremost, intonation cannot become a honed performance skill until a student has achieved a consistent and characteristic tone quality on his or her instrument (refer to *Chapter 6: Tone Quality* in **Teaching Instrumental Music: Developing the COMPLETE Band Program** (2007) Meredith Music Publications, Shelley Jagow). This chapter outlines the many factors affecting tone quality and provides solutions for correcting tonal issues. Until an ensemble can play with good tone quality it is very difficult to approach tuning with any long-term success.

The concept of intonation is directly related to the development of balance and tone. A good tone may be defined as a mature, characteristic sound on the instrument. The characteristic sound of each instrument is determined by the presence of overtones in the sound. Each note is made up of its fundamental frequency along with higher overtone frequencies. It is this harmonic series that determines the characteristic tone color of each instrument. Students must be taught how to produce this correct concept of tone quality for his or her instrument, in order to capture characteristic fundamental tone. When good tone is balanced among all members of the ensemble, then good pitch is a direct result of the product of tone and balance: *In-Tone + In-Balance = In-Tune*

As you explore this book you will find approaches for improving intonation with your ensembles as well as understanding when to appropriately apply various tuning systems in selected repertoire. In addition to extensive alternate fingering charts for each instrument, you will also find blank intonation charts.

# Origin of Common Pitch Tuning Standard A-440

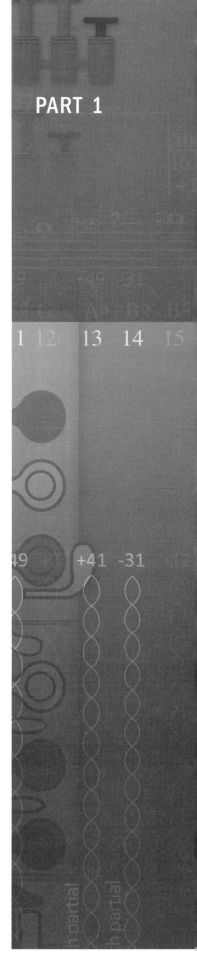

# PART 1

*Ton d'orchestre* (A-434) was the adopted pitch standard near the end of the 18th century with the founding of the Conservatoire. Earlier tuning had mostly endorsed *Ton d'Opéra* (A-409) (Haynes, 2002). In 1858 the French government assigned a commission to establish a uniform musical pitch, led by physicist J. Lissajous, and the mid-430's became this established pitch (Haynes, 2002). The London Philharmonic reached its highest pitch, 455, in 1874 while the British Army Regulation pitch for military bands in 1878 was 452. With the encouragement of a medical doctor and the frustration of vocalists to sing at such a high pitch, England settled on lowering the pitch to 439 and was called the *New Philharmonic Pitch* (Haynes, 2002). This change in pitch forced all orchestral wind players to purchase lower pitched instruments, but the old sharp pitch remained in some British wind-bands. In 1917 the American Federation of Musicians adopted the pitch of 440. Although the adoption of 440 Hz for A was proposed at the Congress at Stuttgart in 1834, it wasn't until 1953 that the International Standardization Organization formally adopted A-440, which has remained the official international standard today. Students and directors need to be aware that they may purchase an instrument at various pitch standards. Please research the specifications of the instrument carefully before you purchase.

## WHY CAN'T ALL INSTRUMENTS BE PITCHED IN C?

If A-440 remains our adopted pitch standard then we can assume that all instruments are tuned to A-440, but some of them are *transposing* instruments while others are *concert pitch* instruments. The clarinet, trumpet and tenor saxophone are transposing instruments in Bb in relation to A at 440, but could also be considered an instrument in C at 392 (Haynes, 2002). A defined pitch standard has placed voices at the level they were originally conceived to sound at their best tone quality. When pitch is shifted, it can often cause difficult tonal problems for some instruments and for voice, especially soprano because higher voices vibrate much faster than lower voices. A singer's vocal register depends on pitch standards, and any changes will affect tone quality and endurance.

An instrument on the other hand can be manufactured at almost any pitch. The tone color of an instrument varies greatly depending on its fundamental pitch. For example, a trumpet in Bb would sound *darker* when compared to the *brightness* of a trumpet in C because it is based on a higher fundamental. If we pitched every instrument in C in relation to A at 440, then we would have to learn a multiple set of fingerings for each instrument. In other words, a saxophonist would have to learn one set of fingerings for the tenor saxophone and another for the alto saxophone. This would be cumbersome and impractical to learn a different set of fingerings within a family of instruments.

# Teaching the Concept of Intonation

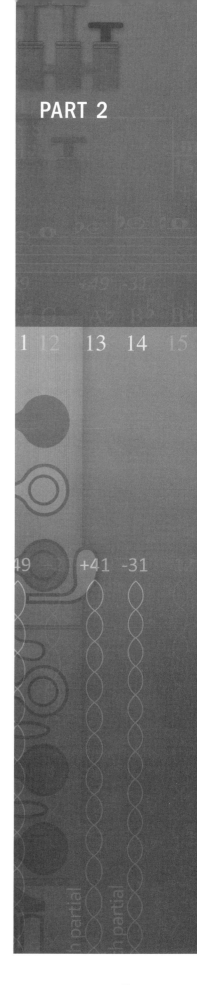

# PART 2

With respect to intonation, such a concept cannot become a performance skill until a student has achieved a consistent and characteristic tone quality on his or her instrument. Teaching towards the three fundamental learning styles can be an effective approach to introducing students to the concept of pitch. The instructional area of intonation can invoke apprehension in the classroom for both the students and the teacher. Pitch may be somewhat more esoteric in impression than the other music fundamentals, and can thus be a challenging concept to teach. We will approach the concept in an attempt to target the foremost student learning styles (verbal, visual, aural, kinesthetic) that can be effective to introducing students to the concept of pitch.

## VERBAL LEARNING STYLE (LEFT-BRAIN)

Pitch may be defined to students by explaining the concept of acoustics. Understanding that a tone is caused by a vibrating air column for wind instruments, a vibrating string for string instruments, or a vibrating membrane, metal, wood, etc. for percussion instruments is the first step in teaching players about simple acoustics.

Five properties of sound (pitch, intensity, timbre, duration, and direction) are outlined in detail in Garafalo's (1996) book *Improving Intonation in Band and Orchestra Performance.* For purposes here, we discuss the property of pitch. The pitch of a tone is determined by the rate of speed of vibrations (called the *frequency*), which is measured in cycles per second. Without getting into too many details, students should be able to understand the concept that varying pitches vibrate at varying frequencies.

If a concert A is sounded by two instruments, yet one instrument sounds A at 440 cps and the second instrument sounds A at 450 cps, then these two instruments will sound out of tune. The varying frequencies clash with one another and the resultant tone is faulty pitch. Therefore, in order to sound in tune, the two instruments must be sounded with identical frequencies.

## VISUAL/AURAL LEARNING STYLE (RIGHT-BRAIN)

Verbal definitions and explanations may be enhanced by the use of drawings on the chalkboard and other visual aids. For example, the pattern of a sound wave may be illustrated on the chalkboard and then further illustrated by having two students hang onto a long rope. One student holds their end of the rope steady, while the second student moves their arm up and down to simulate how a sound wave would look and how it would travel. Varying the speed of the arm movements would correspond to varying pitches or frequencies. A higher pitch will have faster vibrations (therefore more cycles per second), while a lower pitch will have slower vibrations (therefore fewer cycles per second).

Listen for any audible *beats* in the sound of two instruments sounding concert A simultaneously. If you can hear beats, then the sound wave may look something as illustrated in Figure 2.1 due to the irregular frequencies not matching up with each other.

---

**Figure 2.1.** Tonal Waves at Unequal Frequencies

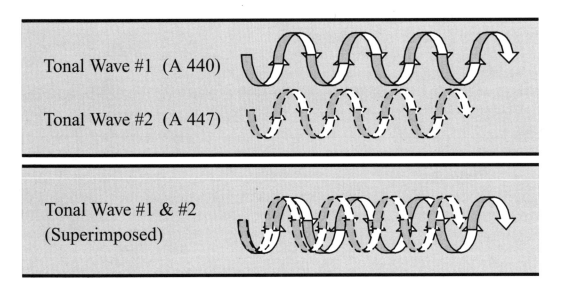

By adjusting embouchure, the students should be able to bring the two tones together to sound *beat-less*. One student should hold their pitch as steady as possible while the second student adjusts their embouchure in an attempt to remove any audible beats between the two tones. If the student must *pinch* or *firm* the embouchure, then their pitch is *flat* to the other tone, and they must therefore *shorten* the length of their instrument. If the student must *loosen* or *relax* the embouchure, then their pitch is *sharp* to the other tone, and they must therefore *lengthen* the length of their instrument. A beat-less sound indicates that the two tones are vibrating at the same frequency (Figure 2.2).

**Figure 2.2.** Tonal Waves at Equal Frequencies

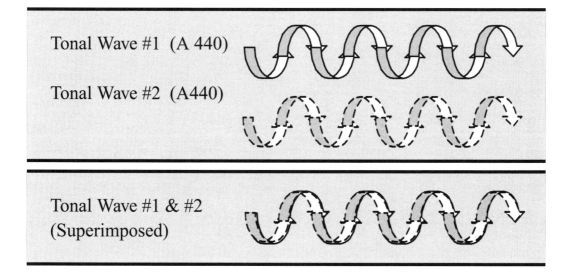

A good rule to remember is: The slower the beats sound the closer they are to matching pitch; and the faster the beats sound the further away they are from matching pitch (Figure 2.3).

**Figure 2.3.** Tonal Waves

As you hear the beats slow down, the two tones are closer to sounding in tune.

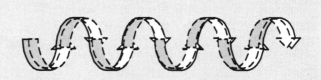

As you hear the beats get faster, the two tones are further away from sounding in tune.

By means of illustration, the teacher may demonstrate what two sound waves look like when superimposed with each other when at identical pitch and when at varying pitches. Such a demonstration would also relate well to a topic on consonant and dissonant intervals. Additionally, an electronic tuner will visually demonstrate to a student when a pitch sounds flat or sharp.

## KINESTHETIC LEARNING STYLE

Students can actively participate in learning the concept of pitch by practicing with an electronic tuner. While playing a note on their instrument, the student should experiment with their embouchure and air speed to hear how such factors affect pitch. Alternate fingerings should also be explored. The student should then practice with a tuner to play each and every note on their instrument as close to *in tune* as possible. This is the best way that a student may begin to learn the specific *pitch tendencies* of their instrument. The fingering charts in this book identify the general tendencies of each instrument by providing the alternate fingering to correct the pitch.

The student should then practice intonation with another student. One method is to have a student play each note on their instrument while the second student observes the tuner and records the number of cents flat or sharp that each pitch is. This record can then be studied by the student to see which particular notes must be played with better attention to pitch. Another method is to have two students of like-instruments play the same note and work towards a *beatless* sound, trying to decrease the amount of time it takes each time to reach the desired *beatless* sound. Instead of listening for whether their pitch is higher or lower than a neighbor's pitch, a student should listen for beats. Once a student becomes quite proficient at these methods, they should repeat the latter procedure with an un-like instrument. This now brings the concept of timbre into the equation which will further mature the player's aural and pitch skills.

# Equal Tempered Tuning versus Just or Pure Interval Tuning

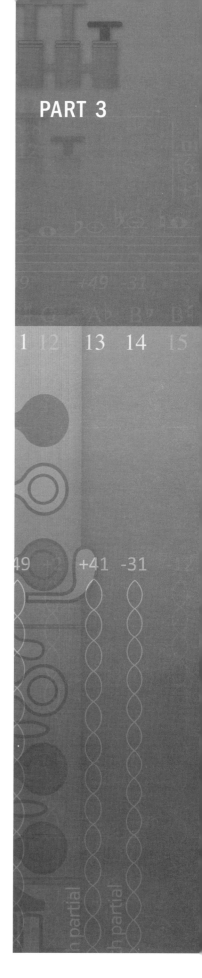

# PART 3

There is a history of many tuning systems that could keep one involved for quite some time with discovering the science and math with each system. However, for our purposes, we essentially need to understand two systems: Equal-Tempered and Just; (a third system that would be pragmatic to understand is Pythagorean Tuning). In fact, the Equal-Tempered tuning is somewhat of a compromise between Just and Pythagorean. Another observation one will notice is that when Pythagorean and Just cent values do not match, they differ by the amount of 22 cents.

Equal tempered tuning is a system that evenly divides the 12 half step intervals in an octave. The system provides a basis for comprehending the measurement of a cent, which is equal to 1/100th of an equal-tempered semitone. Most fixed keyboard instruments are tuned to the equal temperament scale, wind instruments are tuned to Equal Temperament, and most tuners available to the average consumer are tuned to Equal Temperament. However, there are occasions when instrumental ensembles should tune to pure intervals because just intervals sound with increased resonance when compared to equal intervals. This is largely due to the natural properties of intervals found in the harmonic series. The lower the ratio integers, the higher the number of common partials, and thus the more consonant the interval. The higher the ratio integers, the lower the number of common partials, and thus the more dissonant the interval.

You may think life would be much simpler if we could just divide the intervals of a diatonic scale into equal parts. Unfortunately, life isn't that simple. Pizer refers to John Redfield's book (*Music: A Science and an Art*) with an explanation of frequency relationships:

> Dividing the octave into twelve equal parts sound very simple. But the person who takes up the problem expecting to find it easy will be quite likely to drop it like the proverbial hot potato. . . . To determine the notes for any diatonic scale we start with the frequency of its keynote. This we increase by 1/8 of itself; then by 1/9, 1/15, 1/8, 1/9, 1/8 and 1/15, of the successive frequencies. Each frequency is obtained from the preceding one by increasing the latter by some fraction of itself. . . .

> It seems then, that the increases necessary to produce the successive notes of the diatonic scale may be secured by multiplication as well as by addition. And it is increases of this multiplicative kind that have to be made in the case of our even tempered scale; only there will have to be twelve of them, and the increases will all have to be equal—multiplicatively equal. This means that we shall have to find a fraction which will double any number if that number is multiplied by the fraction twelve times. This fraction, if we could find it,

would increase 1 to 2 by multiplying 1 by it twelve times. . . . To put the question into the language of the mathematician, 'What is the twelfth root of 2?'. . . . The number when we find it, correct to six decimal places, is 1.059463. Less than six decimal places are insufficient to give a rule accurate enough to tune the piano (Pizer, 1976, p. 126).

Clear as mud, right? Instruments must be tuned to the equal-tempered scale when manufactured, or else there would need to be a separate instrument required for every key. (This is true for every instrument except trombone and strings.) When the equal-tempered scale is divided into twelve keys in the octave, each instrument can easily modulate to any key without great disruption to the ear. However, to provide the advantage of playing in any key, the instrument's tonality itself will always be a little out of tune because the intervals of the natural diatonic scale are not the same size, as we learned from Redfield in the previous paragraph.

Unfortunately there is no *perfect* tuning system. So when should we use Equal-Tempered Tuning (ET) and when should we use Just Tuning with our ensembles? For most ensembles that engage in a balanced diet of repertoire, they will end up utilizing ET about 90% of the time and JT about 10% of the time. The justification for this selection of tuning systems is outlined in Table 3.1.

**Table 3.1.** Justification for Equal-Tempered Tuning versus Just/Pure Tuning

| Equal Tempered Tuning (ET)<br>*Approximate Usage = 90%* | Just/Pure Tuning (JT)<br>*Approximate Usage = 10%* |
|---|---|
| Most wind band music is largely melodic in nature and thus equal temperament is recommended for pieces of faster tempo, atonal music, and/or many key modulations. | Just tuning should be used when possible in chorales, slower lyrical sections that have sustained cadential points, final chords of any tempo, or any sustained harmony where there is time for the ear to hear *beats*. |
| ET has equal sized seconds (100 cents) that make it impractical for harmonic (vertical) tuning. | JT has different sizes of seconds that make it impractical for melodic (horizontal) tuning. |

The ability to move between equal and just tuning is a skill we want to develop with every player in the ensemble. Regardless of what tuning method is employed, the end result should be one that illustrates excellent musicianship and captures the sound that makes aesthetic sense to the piece.

## INTERVAL RELATIONSHIPS OF TONES

Just Tuning is a result of the natural intervals of pure fifths and thirds as located in the harmonic series. In relation to Equal-tempered Tuning, just fifths are slightly larger, and major thirds are much smaller. To identify interval relationships, it is necessary to understand the harmonic series (Figure 3.1), the relationship of consonance and dissonance in the harmonic series (Table 3.2), and the interval relationships between equal and just tuning (Table 3.3). A cent is equal to 1/100th of a semitone; therefore, each semitone is equal to 100 cents. If an octave is divided equally into 12 steps, then each step in ET will have the value of 100 cents. Therefore, a Perfect Octave has 12 equal steps of 100 cents each, which equals a total of 1200 cents. Using the same formula for the octave, a Perfect 5th is comprised of 7 steps. However, 7 steps in ET will represent the total value of 700 cents, but in reality, the 7 steps in JT will represent the total value of 702 cents. This computes to an interval difference of 2 cents. The ratio of 3:2 for the interval of a Perfect 5th tells us that the third partial of the lower tone has the same cycles per second as the second partial of the upper tone. If we were to actually tune a keyboard instrument to true beatless harmony (pure tuning) then we would end up with an octave that is intolerably out of tune. Equal tempered tuning is necessary for the convenience of playing in all major and minor keys on keyboard instruments.

**Figure 3.1.** Harmonic Series

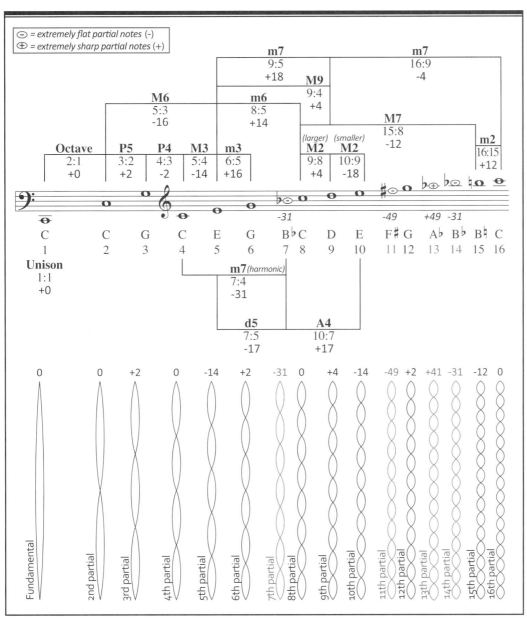

**Note:** The 7th harmonic is the first harmonic *not* to give a note on the normal scale. It is 31 cents flatter than A♯. If notes are played based on this resonance, they will sound badly out of tune with other instruments, so it is not normally used. However, composers have sometimes specifically asked for this resonance to be used for special effect. Vaughan Williams uses it in one of his symphonies and so does Benjamin Britten in the opening movement of his Serenade for Tenor, Horn and Strings. (Bain, p. 42)

**Table 3.2.** Relationship of Consonance and Dissonance in the Harmonic Series

| Partial | Interval (Ratio) | Coinciding Partials (CONSONANCE)* | CONFLICTING Partials (DISSONANCE)* | Notation |
|---------|------------------|------------------------------------|-------------------------------------|----------|
| 1 | Unison (1:1) | 6 | 0 | |
| 2 | Octave (2:1) | 3 | 0 | |
| 3 | Perfect Fifth (3:2) | 2 | 2 whole tones | |
| 4 | Perfect Fourth (4:3) | 1 | 1 semitone 3 whole tones | |
| 5 | Major Third (5:4) | 1 | 2 semitones | |
| 6 | Major Sixth (5:3) | 1 | 2 whole tones | |
| 7 | Minor Third (6:5) | 1 | 1 semitone 1 whole tone | |

- ■ *Dissonance* (conflicting partials) is produced by the quantity of semitone and whole-tone partial conflicts created by the fundamental tones.

- ■ *Consonance* (coinciding partials) is created not only by the interval created by the fundamental tones, but also by the quantity of aligned partials created by each fundamental.

Within the first six partials, the Unison is most consonant with six coinciding harmonies, followed by the Octave with three coinciding harmonies, the Perfect Fifth with two coinciding harmonies, and the Perfect Fourth, Major Third, Major Sixth, and Minor Third each with one coinciding harmony.

**Table 3.3.** Interval Relationships between Equal and Just Tuning

| Ratio | Interval | Interval Notation | Equal Tempered Tuning (in cents) | Pure/Just Interval Tuning (in cents) | Just Interval Difference |
|---|---|---|---|---|---|
| 2:1 | Perfect Octave | | 1200 | 1200 | 0 |
| 15:8 | Major 7th | | 1100 | 1088 | 12 cents flat |
| 9:5<br>16:9<br>7:4 | minor 7th<br>Dominant 7th<br>Harmonic minor 7th | | 1000 | 1018<br>996<br>969 | 18 cents sharp<br>4 cents flat<br>31 cents flat |
| 5:3 | Major 6th | | 900 | 884 | 16 cents flat |
| 8:5<br>25:16 | minor 6th<br>Augmented 5th | | 800 | 814<br>773 | 14 cents sharp<br>27 cents flat |
| 3:2 | Perfect 5th | | 700 | 702 | 2 cents sharp |
| 7:5<br>45:32<br>64:45<br>10:7 | diminished 5th<br>Augmented 4th<br>diminished 5th<br>Augmented 4th | | 600 | 583<br>590<br>610<br>617 | 17 cents flat<br>10 cents flat<br>10 cents sharp<br>17 cents sharp |
| 4:3 | Perfect 4th | | 500 | 498 | 2 cents flat |
| 5:4 | Major 3rd | | 400 | 386 | 14 cents flat |
| 6:5 | Minor 3rd | | 300 | 316 | 16 cents sharp |
| 9:8 | Major 2nd | | 200 | 204 | 4 cents sharp |
| 16:15 | minor 2nd | | 100 | 112 | 12 cents sharp |
| 1:1 | Perfect Unison | | 0 | 0 | 0 |

**Table 3.4.** Interval Adjustment for Perfect and Imperfect Consonances

| | Ratio | Interval |
|---|---|---|
| *Perfect* consonances | 1:1 | Unison |
| | 2:1 | Octave |
| | 3:2 | P5 |
| | 4:3 | P4 |
| *Imperfect* consonances | 5:3 | M6 |
| | 5:4 | M3 |
| | 6:5 | m3 |
| | 8:5 | m6 |

| Adjustments from Equal Temperament to Just Intonation | | | | | | | |
|---|---|---|---|---|---|---|---|
| **Major Scale** | **C** | **D** | **E** | **F** | **G** | **A** | **B** | **C** |
| | 0 | +4 | -14 | -2 | +2 | -16 | -12 | 0 |
| **minor scale** | **C** | **D** | **Eb** | **F** | **G** | **Ab** | **Bb** | **C** |
| | 0 | +4 | +16 | -2 | +2 | +14 | +18 | 0 |

# Intervals Come in Different Sizes

# PART 4

## 5-LIMIT AND 7-LIMIT JUST TUNING

Just tuning can be calculated in a number of different ways depending on the ratio of prime numbers. For the most part, we can serve our purpose of tuning the wind band based on 5-limit tuning (Table 4.1), which uses ratios based on prime numbers 2, 3 and 5. In other words, the largest number in the interval ratio can be no more than a multiple of 5. And we learned earlier that the smaller the ratio interval the more consonant the interval. In 7-limit tuning (Table 4.1) the largest number in the interval ratio can be no more than a multiple of 7, thus using prime numbers 2, 3, 5 and 7. Just tuning can move even higher into the harmonic series using complicated prime ratios of 11, 13, 17, 19 and beyond.

**Table 4.1.** 5-Limit and 7-Limit Tuning

| 5-Limit | | | 7-Limit |
|---|---|---|---|
| 1:1 | 0 | Unison | 1:1 |
| 16:15 | +12 | minor 2nd | 16:15 |
| 10:9 | -18 | Major 2nd (small) | 10:9 |
| 9:8 | +4 | Major 2nd (large) | 9:8 |
| 6:5 | +16 | minor 3rd | 6:5 |
| 5:4 | -14 | Major 3rd | 5:4 |
| 4:3 | -2 | Perfect 4th | 4:3 |
| | **-17** | **Diminished 5th** | **7:5** |
| 45:32 | -10 | Augmented 4th | 45:32 |
| 64:45 | +10 | Diminished 5th | 64:45 |
| | **+17** | **Augmented 4th** | **10:7** |
| 3:2 | +2 | Perfect 5th | 3:2 |
| 8:5 | +14 | minor 6th | 8:5 |
| 5:3 | -16 | Major 6th | 5:3 |
| | **-31** | **minor 7th** (harmonic) | **7:4** |
| 16:9 | -4 | minor 7th (small) | 16:9 |
| 9:5 | +18 | minor 7th (large) | 9:5 |
| 15:8 | -12 | Major 7th | 15:8 |
| 2:1 | 0 | Octave | 2:1 |

## THE SUPERTONIC SECOND

When we look at the harmonic series again, we also see there are different sizes of the major and minor second intervals (Figure 4.1); each with a different ratio and different interval width.

If we tune the minor 2nd to ratio 17:16, then we must raise the 2nd by 5 cents.

If we tune the minor 2nd to ratio 16:15, then we must raise the 2nd by 12 cents.

If we tune the major 2nd to ratio 10:9, then we must lower the 2nd by 18 cents.

If we tune the major 2nd to ratio 9:8, then we must raise the 2nd by 4 cents.

**Figure 4.1.** Major and Minor Second Sizes

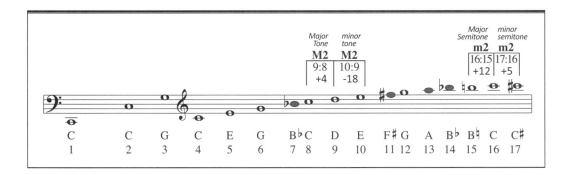

The construction of the diatonic major scale (Table 4.2) is made up of the first three sizes of seconds found in the harmonic series:

T = Major Tone (9:8) = 204 cents

t = minor tone (10:9) = 182 cents

s = Major Semitone (16:15) = 112 cents

**Table 4.2.** Construction of a Just Diatonic Major Scale

| Diatonic Major Scale | | | | | | | | |
|---|---|---|---|---|---|---|---|---|
| **NOTE** | **C** | **D** | **E** | **F** | **G** | **A** | **B** | **C** |
| Solfege | Do | Re | Mi | Fa | So | La | Ti | Do |
| Scale Degree | Tonic | Supertonic | Mediant | Sub-Dominant | Dominant | Sub-Mediant | Leading Tone | Tonic |
| Step | | T | t | s | T | t | T | s |
| Ratio | | 9:8 | 10:9 | 16:15 | 9:8 | 10:9 | 9:8 | 16:15 |
| Cents | | 204 | 182 | 112 | 204 | 182 | 204 | 112 |

Although the diatonic major scale uses only one size of minor second, it uses two sizes of major second:

**Table 4.3.** Size of Major Second

| Size of Major Second | | | |
|---|---|---|---|
| large M2 (9:8) 204 cents | C-D (Do-Re) | F-G (Fa-So) | A-B (La-Ti) |
| small M2 (10:9) 182 cents | D-E (Re-Mi) | G-A (So-La) | |

We also see that the supertonic ii chord is not constructed with a just perfect fifth (3/2; 702 cents) (Table 4.4) like all the other major and minor chords. Rather, a *wolf fifth* (40/27; 680 cents) is found at the interval of a fifth from supertonic D. Theorists have attempted several methods to try and move the *bad* supertonic to a different position in the scale, but the problem does not disappear; it merely moves to a different position. Thus, the lesser of all evils is to leave the supertonic as it is. As a result, the ii chord is more dissonant than iii or vi because of the dissonant nature of its minor third (Table 4.5), being 22 cents smaller than a Just minor third.

**Table 4.4.**  Just Perfect Fifths in Major and Minor Chords with Exception of ii Chord

| Diatonic Major Scale | | | | | | |
|---|---|---|---|---|---|---|
| Major & minor chords | I | *ii* | **iii** | **IV** | **V** | **vi** |
| Perfect fifth | C-G | *D-A* | E-B | F-C | G-D | A-E |
| Cents | 702 | *680* | 702 | 702 | 702 | 702 |

**Table 4.5.**  Triad Construction in a Just Diatonic Major Scale

| Diatonic Major Scale Triad Construction | | | | | | | | |
|---|---|---|---|---|---|---|---|---|
| **NOTE** | **C** | **D** | **E** | **F** | **G** | **A** | **B** | **C** |
| Ratio | 1:1 | 9:8 | 5:4 | 4:3 | 3:2 | 5:3 | 15:8 | 2:1 |
| Cents | 0 | 204 | 386 | 498 | 702 | 884 | 1088 | 1200 |
| Triad | CEG | **DFA** | EGB | FAC | GBD | ACE | BDF | CEG |
| Scale Degree | I | **ii** | iii | IV | V | vi | vii° | VIII/I |

C–E = M3 = Tt = 386 cents [Just M3 = 5:4]

**D–F = m3 = ts = 294 cents [this m3 is 22 cents smaller than Just m3; ratio is actually 32:27]**

E–G = m3 = sT = 316 cents [Just m3 = 6:5]

F–A = M3 = Tt = 386 cents [Just M3 = 5:4]

G–B = M3 = tT = 386 cents [Just M3 = 5:4]

A–C = m3 = Ts = 316 cents [Just m3 = 6:5]

## THE MINOR SEVENTH

When we look at the harmonic series again, we see that there is not one, but three minor 7th intervals (Figure 4.2). And although each interval is indeed a minor 7th, each has a different ratio and thus a different interval width.

If we tune the minor 7th to ratio 16:9, then we must lower the 7th by 4 cents.

If we tune the minor 7th to ratio 9:5, then we must raise the 7th by 18 cents.

If we tune the minor 7th to ratio 7:4, then we must lower the 7th by 31 cents.

This can make it confusing to understand which interval width to use when tuning the ensemble with Just Tuning. In addition, the minor seventh chord is often heard as a major triad with an added sixth. The answer to tuning the seventh essentially depends on context of melody and harmony, and shared tones within the harmonic progression.

**Figure 4.2.** Minor Seventh Sizes

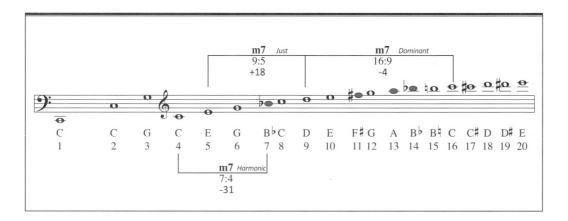

Typically the seventh in a nondominant seventh chord (mm7) will be tuned to the ratio 9:5 (+18 cents). But when we deal with dominant seventh chords (Mm7) the seventh will have variations in tuning dependent on context. A summary of choices for selecting the interval size of the seventh in dominant seventh chords is summarized in Table 4.6.

1. 1:1 5:4 3:2 **16:9** when the chord functions as a dissonance and wants to resolve

2. 1:1 5:4 3:2 **9:5** can also work well as a dissonant function

3. 1:1 5:4 3:2 **7:4** when the chord functions more as a consonance; stability

**Table 4.6.** minor-seventh (m7) intervals in a Dominant Seventh Chord

| | | minor-seventh (m7) intervals in a Dominant Seventh chord | | |
|---|---|---|---|---|
| **Interval** | **Cents** | **Difference** | **Ratio** | **Recommended Usage** |
| JT-m7 | 969 | 31 cents ♭ | 7:4 <br><br> 1:1 = Root <br> 5:4 = M3 <br> 3:2 = P5 <br> **7:4 = m7** | This tuning falls in the 7th partial which is so flat that it is often impractical, or impossible, for some instruments to adjust this amount (31 cents). However, this is a more consonant tuning and has greater stability than the other choices. [This is the tuning preferred by jazz players and barbershop quartets.] Although a consonant chord, it still resolves well. This tuning is best reserved for dominant harmonic functions (Mm7). |
| JT-m7 | 996 | 4 cents ♭ | 16:9 <br><br> 1:1 = Root <br> 5:4 = M3 <br> 3:2 = P5 <br> **16:9 = m7** | Best used when the chord functions as a dissonance and wants to resolve. The 16:9 dominant tuning is found naturally in the just diatonic major scale. This tuning also works best when following a subdominant chord (IV). |
| ET-m7 | 1000 | 0 | | |
| JT-m7 | 1018 | 18 cents ♯ | 9:5 <br><br> 1:1 = Root <br> 5:4 = M3 <br> 3:2 = P5 <br> **9:5 = m7** | This tuning is more dissonant and can also work well in resolutions. It works best when following a supertonic chord (ii). |

## THE TRITONE

The tritone is just what the name implies—three tones—three whole tones to be precise in conventional theory—the equivalent of half of an octave. In equal-tempered tuning a whole tone is equal to 200 cents; thus a tritone equals the interval distance of 600 cents. The tritone may be called an augmented-fourth or the enharmonic name of a diminished fifth. However, in just tuning, an augmented fourth and a diminished fifth are two very different intervals. There are also several sizes of the just tritone as follows (Table 4.7):

**Table 4.7.** Tritone Sizes

| TriTone Sizes | | | | | |
|---|---|---|---|---|---|
| 31 cents ♯ | G♭ | 631 | 36:25 | diminished 5th | d5 |
| 31 cents ♭ | F♯ | 569 | 25:18 | Augmented 4th | A4 |
| 17 cents ♯ | G♭ | 617 | 10:7 | diminished 5th | d5 |
| 17 cents ♭ | F♯ | 583 | 7:5 | Augmented 4th | A4 |
| 10 cents ♯ | G♭ | 610 | 64:45 | diminished 5th | d5 |
| 10 cents ♭ | F♯ | 590 | 45:32 | Augmented 4th | A4 |

Table 4.8 provides a more in-depth illustration of equal and just tuning with corresponding frequencies and interval sizes.

**Table 4.8.** Equal and Just Tuning Frequencies, Harmonics, and Interval Sizes

| Harmonic | Cents Deviation from ET | Note | ET (cents) | ET Frequency (Decimal) | ET Frequency (Hz) | JT Frequency (cents) | JT Frequency (Ratio) | JT Frequency (Decimal) | JT Frequency (Hz) | Interval | |
|---|---|---|---|---|---|---|---|---|---|---|---|
| 1:2:4:8:16 | In Tune | C | 1200 | 2.00 | 523.26 | 1200 | 2:1 | 2.00 | 523.26 | Octave | P8 |
| 15:30 | 12 cents b | B | 1100 | 1.89 | 493.89 | 1088 | 15:8 | 1.88 | 490.47 | Major 7th | M7 |
| | 18 cents # | Bb | 1000 | 1.78 | 466.17 | 1018 | 9:5 | 1.80 | 471.04 | minor 7th (large) | m7 |
| | 4 cents b | Bb | 1000 | 1.78 | 466.17 | 996 | 16:9 | 1.78 | 465.09 | minor 7th (small) | m7 |
| 7:14:28 | 31 cents b | Bb | | | | 969 | 7:4 | 1.75 | 457.89 | minor 7th (harmonic) | m7 |
| 27 | 16 cents b | A | 900 | 1.68 | 440.00 | 884 | 5:3 | 1.67 | 436 | Major 6th | M6 |
| 13:26 | 14 cents # | Ab | 800 | 1.59 | 415.31 | 814 | 8:5 | 1.60 | 418.68 | minor 6th | m6 |
| 3:6:12:24 | 2 cents # | G | 700 | 1.50 | 392.00 | 702 | 3:2 | 1.50 | 392.45 | Perfect 5th | P5 |
| 23 | 31 cents # | Gb | 600 | 1.41 | 369.99 | 631 | 36:25 | 1.44 | 376.68 | diminished 5th | d5 |
| 11:22 | 31 cents b | F# | 600 | 1.41 | 369.99 | 569 | 25:18 | 1.39 | 363.43 | Augmented 4th | A4 |
| 23 | 17 cents # | Gb | 600 | 1.41 | 369.99 | 617 | 10:7 | 1.43 | 373.64 | diminished 5th | d5 |
| 11:22 | 17 cents b | F# | 600 | 1.41 | 369.99 | 583 | 7:5 | 1.40 | 366.37 | Augmented 4th | A4 |
| 23 | 10 cents # | Gb | 600 | 1.41 | 369.99 | 610 | 64:45 | 1.42 | 372.14 | diminished 5th | d5 |
| 11:22 | 10 cents b | F# | 600 | 1.41 | 369.99 | 590 | 45:32 | 1.41 | 367.87 | Augmented 4th | A4 |
| 21 | 2 cents b | F | 500 | 1.33 | 349.23 | 498 | 4:3 | 1.33 | 348.83 | Perfect 4th | P4 |
| 5:10:20 | 14 cents b | E | 400 | 1.26 | 329.63 | 386 | 5:4 | 1.25 | 326.98 | Major 3rd | M3 |
| 19 | 16 cents # | Eb | 300 | 1.19 | 311.13 | 316 | 6:5 | 1.20 | 314.01 | minor 3rd | m3 |
| 9:18 | 4 cents # | D | 200 | 1.12 | 293.66 | 204 | 9:8 | 1.13 | 294.34 | Major 2nd (large) | M2 |
| | 18 cents b | D | 200 | 1.12 | 293.66 | 182 | 10:9 | 1.11 | 290.62 | Major 2nd (small) | M2 |
| 17 | 12 cents # | Db | 100 | 1.06 | 277.18 | 112 | 16:15 | 1.07 | 279.10 | minor 2nd | m2 |
| 1:2:4:8:16 | In Tune | C | 0 | 1.00 | 261.63 | 0 | 1:1 | 1.00 | 261.63 | Unison | P1 |

# 14 Steps for Tuning Chords

# PART 5

A constructed Just Intonation Chart for intervals (Figure 5.1) and chords (Figure 5.2) serves as a useful reference for ensemble tuning of chords. An ensemble chord will sound in tune when the proper frequencies are sounded based on the root of the chord. All of the chords illustrated in the *Just Intonation Chart* are based on root C, but the pitch adjustments illustrated will occur on each of the twelve equal tempered roots. The symbol (+) indicates a pitch correction by raising the pitch of the note from equal-tempered tuning, while the symbol (–) indicates a pitch correction by lowering the pitch of the note from equal-tempered tuning.

For example, in a Major chord, all players sounding the Root must play at equal temperament (or zero pitch on a tuner). All players sounding the Major 3rd must lower the pitch by 14 cents, and those sounding the Perfect 5th must raise the pitch by 2 cents. Players should listen for *beats* as a guide to making the necessary adjustments as illustrated. A *beatless* chord will sound more consonant and therefore in tune. A chord played with equal temperament will produce slight *beats* and will sound slightly dissonant and therefore out of tune.

1. Tune simplest and purest intervals first:

    a. Roots and any octave doublings

    b. Perfect 5ths and 4ths

2. Tune more complex intervals last:

    a. Major and minor 3rds

    b. Major and minor 7ths

| Chord Quality | | | |
|---|---|---|---|
| **Consonant** | | **Dissonant** | |
| Perfect | Imperfect | Half-step alterations of perfect intervals | Intervals of 2nd, 7th, and 9th |
| Unison<br>Octave<br>Fifth<br>Fourth | Major third<br>Minor third<br>Major sixth<br>Minor sixth | Augmented fourth<br>Diminished fifth<br>(tritone) | Major second<br>Minor second<br>Major seventh<br>Minor seventh<br>Major ninth<br>Minor ninth |

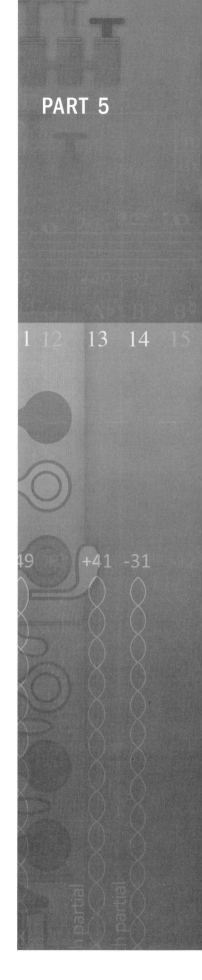

3. Just tuning ultimately depends upon context (harmonic and melodic), function (consonance or dissonance), and aesthetic goals.

4. Tune roots, fifths and then thirds before tuning other intervals.

5. The perfect fifth (P5) is always tuned to the ratio 3:2

6. The major third (M3) is always tuned to the ratio 5:4

7. The minor third (m3) is always tuned to the ratio 6:5

8. The perfect fourth (P4) is always tuned to the ratio 4:3

9. A major triad is always tuned to the ratios 1:1 5:4 3:2

| Major Triad (I) | | | |
|---|---|---|---|
| NOTE | C | E | G |
| Ratio | 1:1 | 5:4 | 3:2 |
| Adjustment (in cents) | 0 | -14 | +2 |

10. A minor triad is always tuned to the ratios 1:1 6:5 3:2. (Tuned to the ratios where it is found as the upper three notes of a major 7th chord; this places its root as a major third above the fundamental.)

| minor Triad (i) | | | |
|---|---|---|---|
| NOTE | C | Eb | G |
| Ratio | 1:1 | 6:5 | 3:2 |
| Adjustment (in cents) | 0 | +16 | +2 |

11. A major seventh chord is always tuned to the ratios 1:1 5:4 3:2 15:8 (The diagram below illustrates that these ratios also work well in keeping the stacking of just tuned thirds.)

| Major Seventh Chord (I⁷) | | | | | | | | | |
|---|---|---|---|---|---|---|---|---|---|
| B | Seventh | | | M7 15:8 | B | 1088 | | | M3 386 |
| G | Fifth | | P5 3:2 | | G | 702 | | m3 316 | |
| E | Third | M3 5:4 | | | E | 386 | M3 386 | | |
| C | Root | | | | C | 0 | | | |

12. A minor seventh chord is always tuned to the ratios 1:1 6:5 3:2 9:5

13. Tuning chord progressions can be complicated when ii or IV is involved due to common tones shared. The director must make an aesthetic decision with tuning, and one that is practical for wind instruments and fixed keyboard instruments that may be prominent in the chord. Some principles to consider when dealing with chord progressions versus isolated chords include:

   a. A minor ii chord can be tuned to 10:9 4:3 5:3 versus 1:1 6:5 3:2

| minor Second Chord (ii) | | | | | | |
|---|---|---|---|---|---|---|
| 5:3 | -16 | vi | A | P5 | +2 | 3:2 |
| 4:3 | -2 | IV | F | m3 | +16 | 6:5 |
| 10:9 | -18 | ii | D | tonic | 0 | 1:1 |

b.   A major IV chord can be tuned to 4:3 5:3 2:1 versus 1:1 5:4 3:2

| Major Fourth Chord (IV) | | | | | | |
|---|---|---|---|---|---|---|
| 2:1 | 0 | I | **C** | P5 | +2 | 3:2 |
| 5:3 | -16 | vi | **A** | M3 | -14 | 5:4 |
| 4:3 | -2 | **IV** | **F** | tonic | 0 | 1:1 |

c.   You have a contextual and aesthetic choice with the minor seventh ratio.

d.   Remember that Augmented intervals will want to resolve UP (outward) and diminished intervals will want to resolve DOWN (inward). Therefore, tune in the direction of the resolution.

14.   A dominant seventh chord is best tuned to the following ratios and contexts:

a.   1:1 5:4 3:2 **7:4** (-31) is best used as a dominant (V) function for all Mm7 chords. It is more consonant than the other two ratios and can be used when resolution is not required in the chord progression. However, even though it is a consonant interval it still provides an energy for resolution.

b.   1:1 5:4 3:2 **16:9** (-4) is best used as a subdominant (IV) function.

c.   1:1 5:4 3:2 **9:5** (+18) can also work well as a dominant function.

## BEST PRACTICE FOR PLAYING IN-TUNE

1.   **Listen** to *good* artists and *good* music daily.

2.   **Practice** your instrument daily using *efficient* practice techniques. Simple amassing of hours does not guarantee success.

3.   Mature your sound to develop a **characteristic tone quality**. (Refer to *Chapter 6: Tone Quality* in *Teaching Instrumental Music: Developing the Complete Band Program* (2007) Meredith Music Publications by Shelley Jagow for extensive information on developing tone quality.)

4.   Develop your ear training. You must be able to easily hear intonation problems. Understand **what needs adjusting**.

5.   Study with a private professional instructor whenever possible. Understand **how to adjust the pitch** to make the best correction for the situation and context.

6.   Keep your instrument in excellent playing condition, and perform on a **quality instrument (mouthpiece/**headjoint/**bocal/reed)**.

**Figure 5.1.** Just Intonation Chart: Intervals

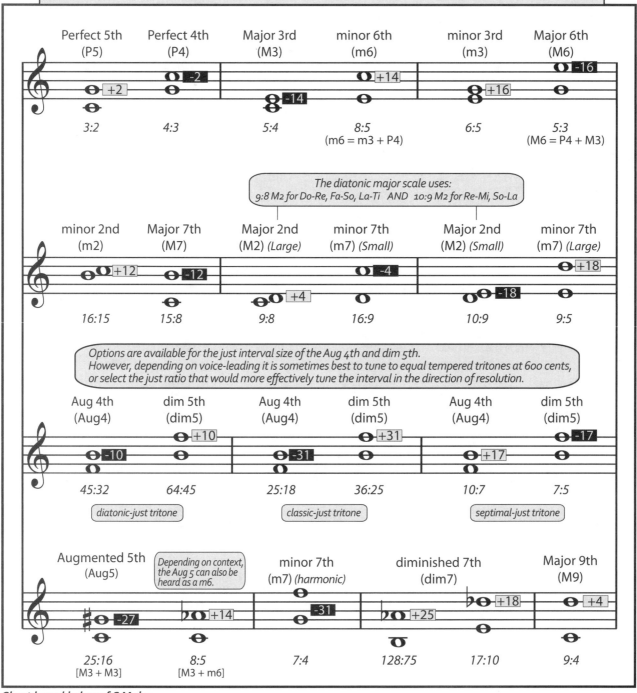

Chart based in key of C Major

**Figure 5.2.** Just Intonation Chart: Chords

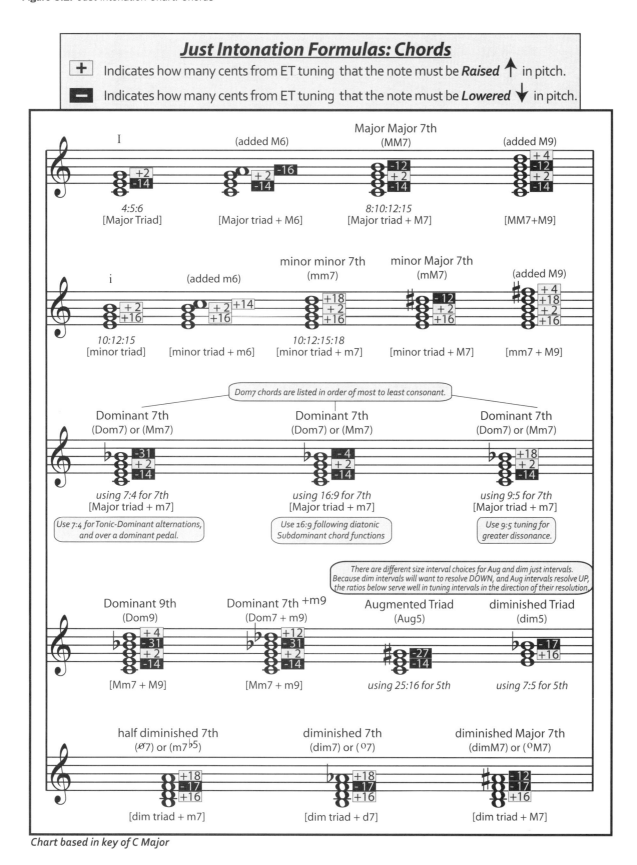

*Chart based in key of C Major*

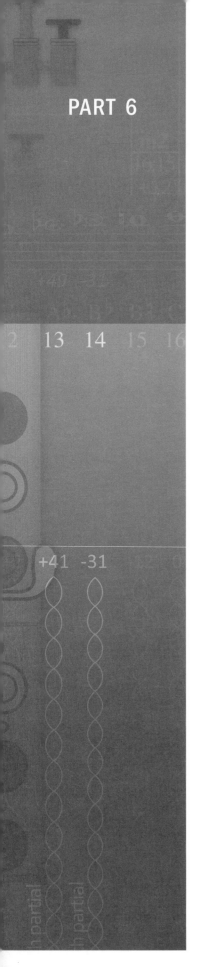

# PART 6

# Fingering Charts Illustrating Pitch Tendency and Suggested Alterations

To purchase and download **legal** copies go to http://www.halleonard.com/meredith-tuning-for-wind-instruments-fingering-charts

**DISCLAIMER:** If you have read this far in the book then you are aware that intonation on wind instruments is affected by many, MANY factors. The following fingering charts are intended to serve as only one of several *tools* for correcting poor intonation. There is no hard and fast rule for correcting poor intonation, but if I had to choose one it would be *use what works best!* There are numerous variations among a player's embouchure, use (or misuse) of air, concept of tone and timbre, instrument quality, mouthpiece shape, bocal length, reed condition, etc. that it would be impossible to prescribe a *one size fits all* approach to intonation. Every player, with assistance from a private instructor and/or band director, must essentially determine *what works best for them.* One of the best means for performing with good intonation is to develop your EAR—mature pitch discernment skills through some of the exercises discussed in this book, and by spending time performing in chamber ensembles with your friends.

## FINGERING CHARTS

**Figure 6.1.** Flute Fingering Chart

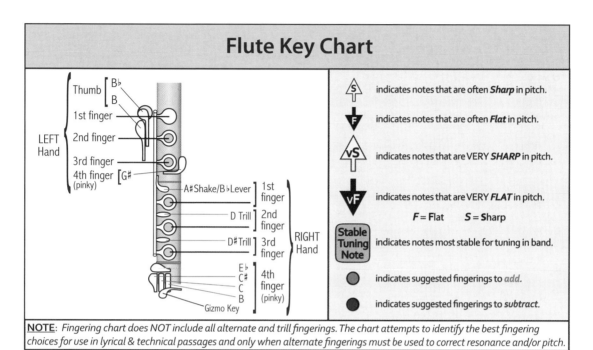

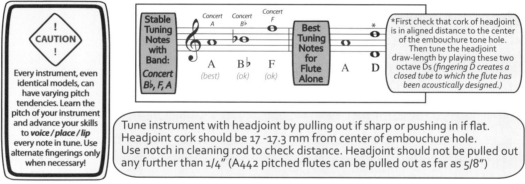

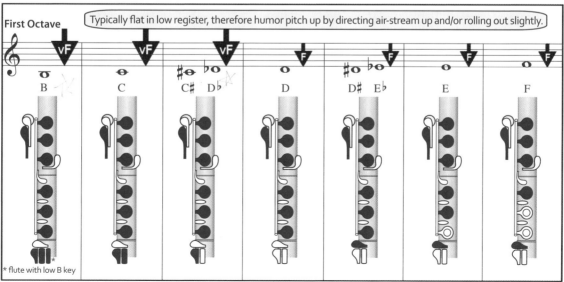

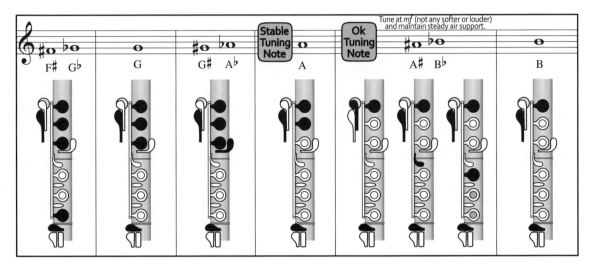

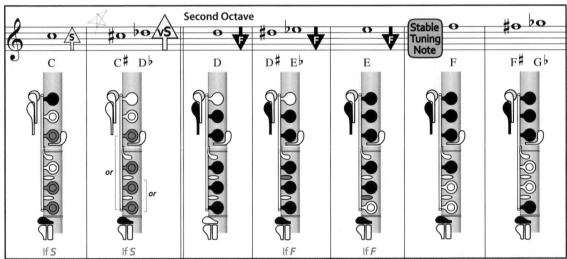

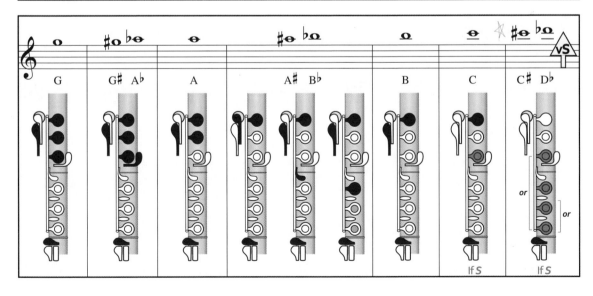

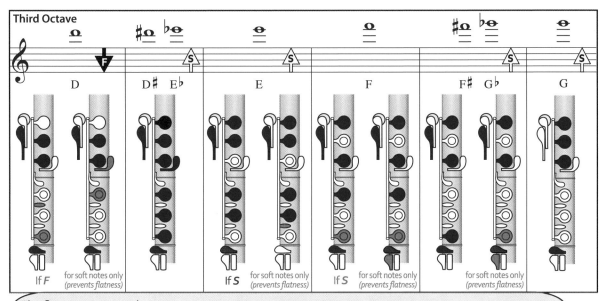

The flute is an *open tube*.
The first octave is produced by the fundamental (first partial) vibration of the pipe; vibrates in *one part*.
The second octave is produced by the second partial; vibrates in *two parts*, and
the third octave is produced by by the third and fourth partials; vibrates in *four parts*.

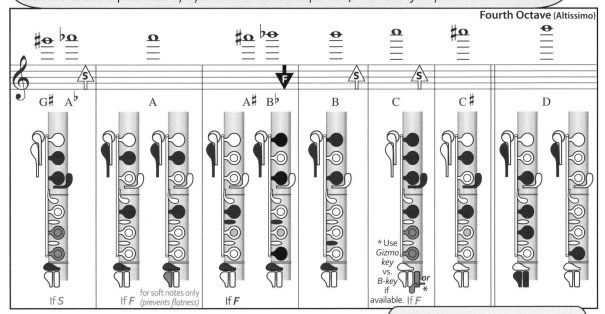

**General Note:**

The more fingers *down* on a regular fingering, the *flatter* the pitch.

The more fingers *up* on a regular fingering, the *sharper* the pitch.

To ▼ pitch, one can **add** any finger, after the first open hole, in first two octaves.

To ⬆ pitch, one can **come off** to just the ring of the key (on an open-hole flute).

Gizmo Key
A small raised lever mounted on the low B key arm to facilitate the individual closing of the low B key. Also known as "high C facilitator"; this lever helps in producing clearer 4th octave C.

Harmonic Fingerings
If harmonic fingerings are used to play notes in the higher register the pitch will be flat. It is suggested to only use harmonic fingerings when conventional fingerings are impractical.

**Figure 6.2.** Oboe Fingering Chart

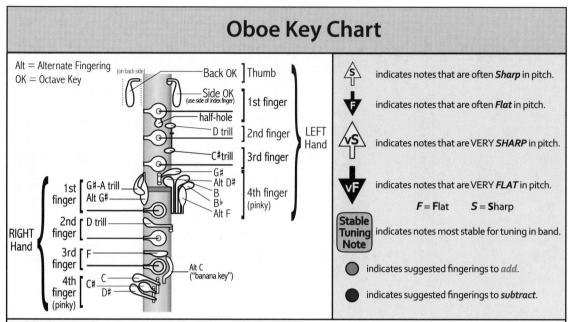

# Oboe Key Chart

Alt = Alternate Fingering
OK = Octave Key

Back OK ] Thumb
Side OK (use side of index finger) ] 1st finger
half-hole
D trill ] 2nd finger
C#trill ] 3rd finger
G#
Alt D#
B
B♭  ] 4th finger
Alt F

1st finger  G#-A trill
Alt G#
2nd finger  D trill
3rd finger  F
4th finger (pinky)  C#  Alt C ("banana key")
C
D#

LEFT Hand

RIGHT Hand

(S) indicates notes that are often **Sharp** in pitch.

(F) indicates notes that are often **Flat** in pitch.

(vS) indicates notes that are VERY **SHARP** in pitch.

(vF) indicates notes that are VERY **FLAT** in pitch.

*F* = Flat     *S* = Sharp

Stable Tuning Note  indicates notes most stable for tuning in band.

⚪ indicates suggested fingerings to *add*.

⚫ indicates suggested fingerings to *subtract*.

**NOTE**: *Fingering chart does NOT include all alternate and trill fingerings. The chart attempts to identify the best fingering choices for use in lyrical & technical passages and only when alternate fingerings must be used to correct resonance and/or pitch.*

**To correct sharpness in pitch**:
1. Relax lips and pull chin down and flat; lips still puckered, but with less firmness; (vowel = ***pooh***)
2. Open up the inside of mouth to reduce *biting;* (vowel = ***aw***)
3. Stay towards the tip of reed.
   The more lip in contact with the reed, the sharper you force the reed to play.

**To correct flatness in pitch**: (make sure reed is pushed in all the way), then:
1. Use faster, focused air; maintain air support and aim air forward and higher in mouth (vowel = ***ee***)
2. Firm the lips; use a smaller lip opening and press lip corners *in* to sides of reed.
3. Take more reed in mouth; more lips in contact with reed. (Lifting oboe *up and in* also accomplishes this.)

**If *consistently* sharp in pitch**:
1. Is embouchure too tight or pinching?
2. Are you taking too much reed into the mouth?

**If *consistently* flat in pitch**:
1. Is embouchure too loose?
2. Are you taking enough reed into the mouth?

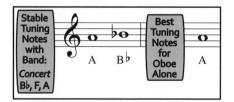

Stable Tuning Notes with Band: Concert B♭, F, A

A   B♭

Best Tuning Notes for Oboe Alone

A

Oboists require a good embouchure and a balanced, quality reed to play with good pitch and tone.
The oboe reed should always be pushed completely in the reed receptor cup initially.
Only minute adjustment (1/4″ at most) by pulling out/pushing in of reed should ever be used, if at all.

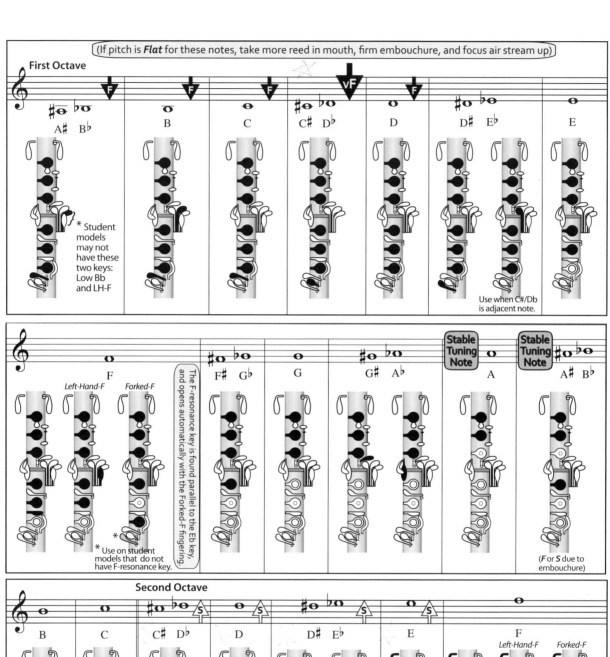

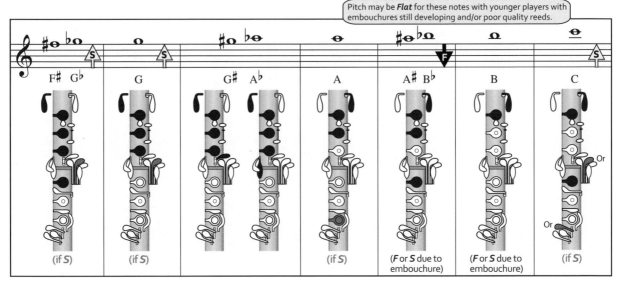

Pitch may be *Flat* for these notes with younger players with embouchures still developing and/or poor quality reeds.

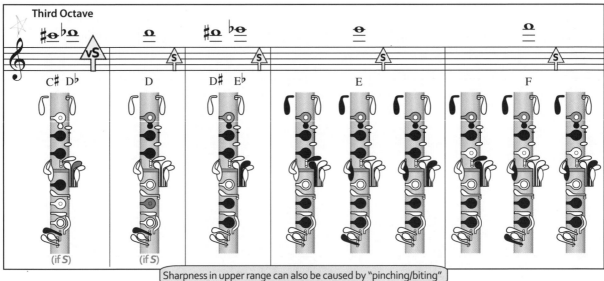

Third Octave

Sharpness in upper range can also be caused by "pinching/biting"

if *F*, take more reed in mouth, firm embouchure, and focus air stream up.

if *S*, take less reed in mouth, relax embouchure, and focus air stream down.

!CAUTION!

Every instrument, even identical models, can have varying pitch tendencies. Learn the pitch of your instrument and advance your skills to *voice / place / lip* every note in tune. Use alternate fingerings only when necessary!

Practice reed "crows" for pitch-embouchure flexibility.

Never play on an old reed; a student reed typically lasts 2 1/2 weeks.

**Figure 6.3.** Clarinet Fingering Chart

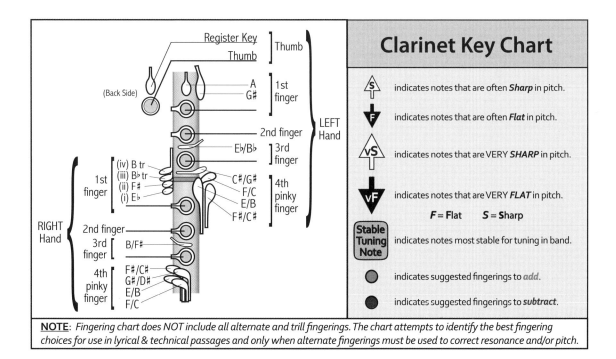

**NOTE**: *Fingering chart does NOT include all alternate and trill fingerings. The chart attempts to identify the best fingering choices for use in lyrical & technical passages and only when alternate fingerings must be used to correct resonance and/or pitch.*

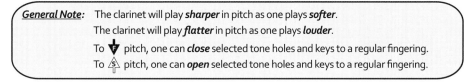

*General Note:*   The clarinet will play **sharper** in pitch as one plays **softer**.
The clarinet will play **flatter** in pitch as one plays **louder**.
To ▼ pitch, one can **close** selected tone holes and keys to a regular fingering.
To ▲ pitch, one can **open** selected tone holes and keys to a regular fingering.

! CAUTION !

Every instrument, even identical models, can have varying pitch tendencies. Learn the pitch of your instrument and advance your skills to *voice / lip / place* every note in tune. Use alternate fingerings only when necessary!

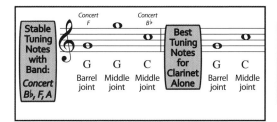

**If *consistently* sharp in pitch**:
1. Is embouchure too tight?
2. Is reed strength too hard?
3. Is barrel length too short?

**If *consistently* flat in pitch**:
1. Is embouchure too loose?
2. Is reed strength too soft?
3. Is barrel length too long?

**To correct sharpness in pitch**:
1. Relax embouchure; pull chin muscles downwards, and bring corners of mouth in toward mouthpiece.
2. Open up the inside of mouth; [Analogies: a) drop floor of mouth,
    b) stretch nostrils downward as if trying to push upper lip into top of mouthpiece.

**To correct flatness in pitch**:
1. Firmer embouchure; more lower lip compression by bringing lower jaw forward.
2. Focus air with energy; increase air support and aim air forward and higher in mouth.

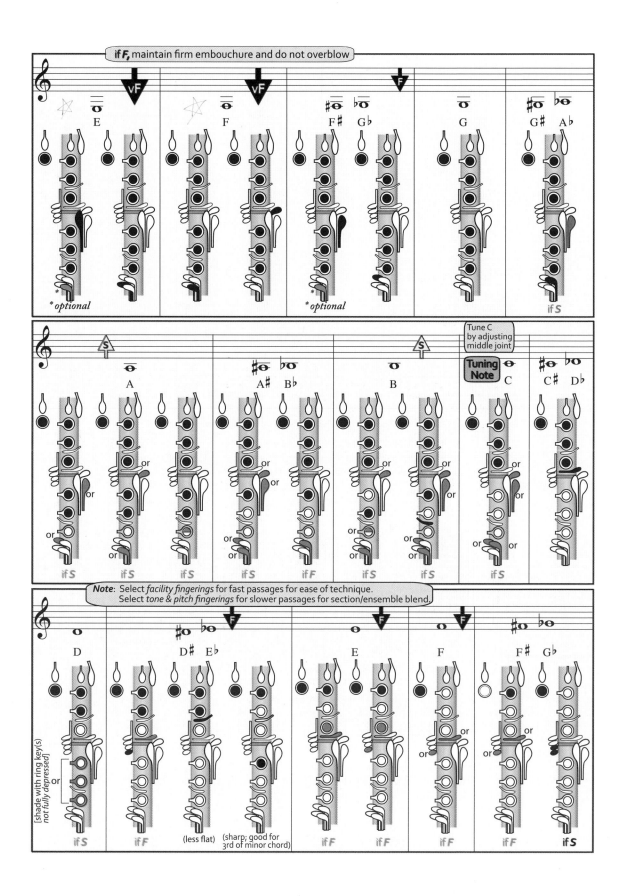

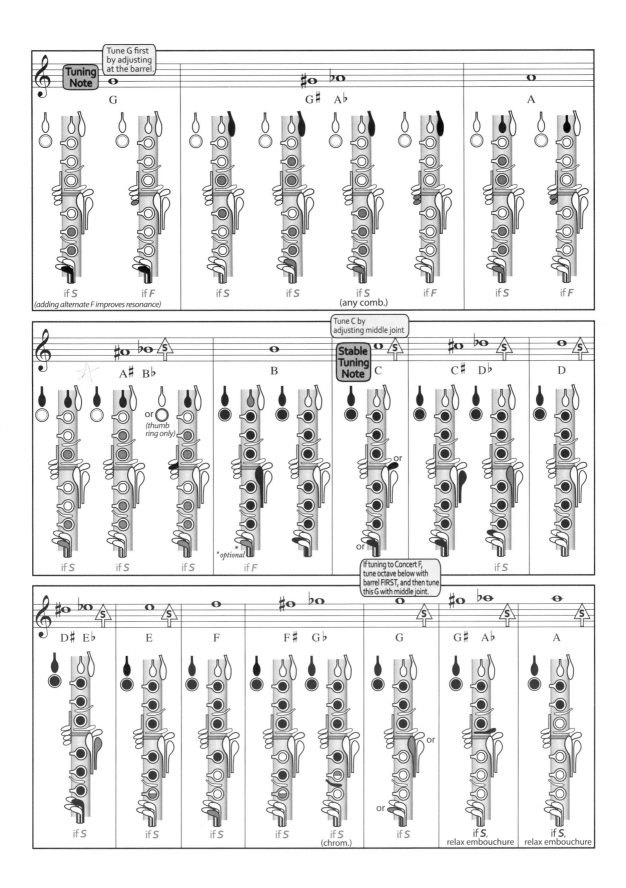

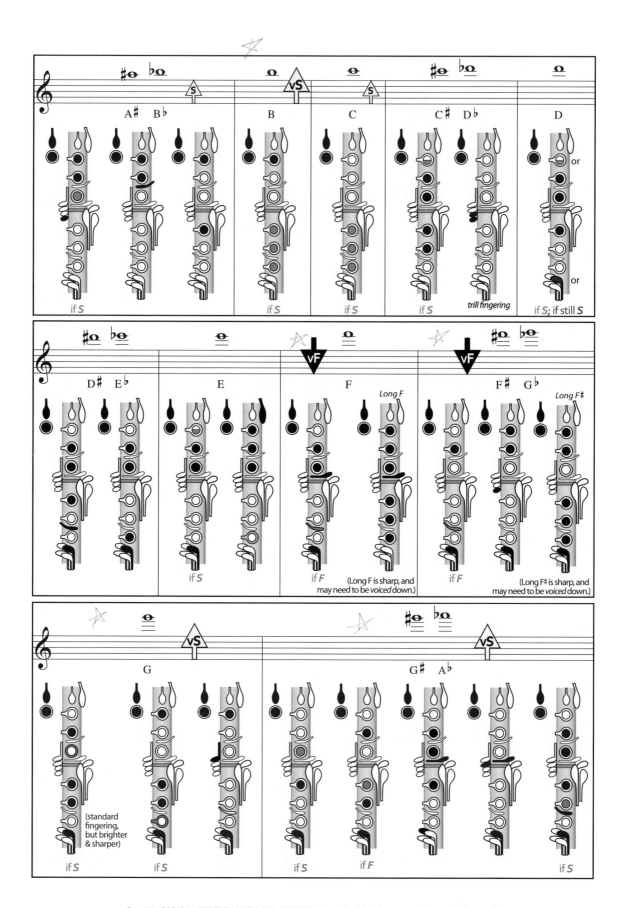

**Figure 6.4.** Saxophone Fingering Chart

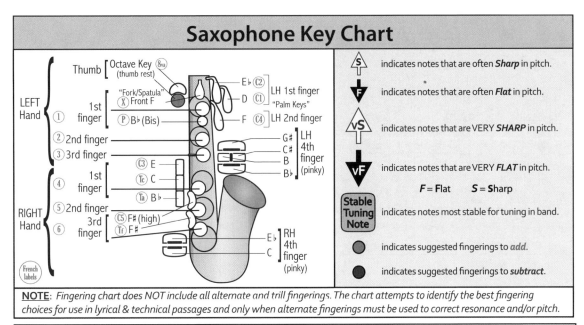

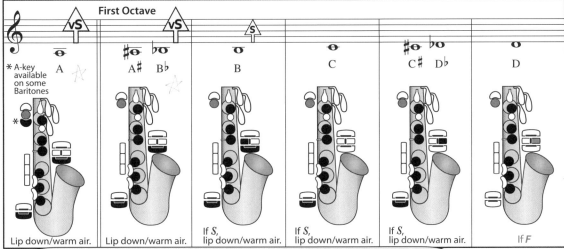

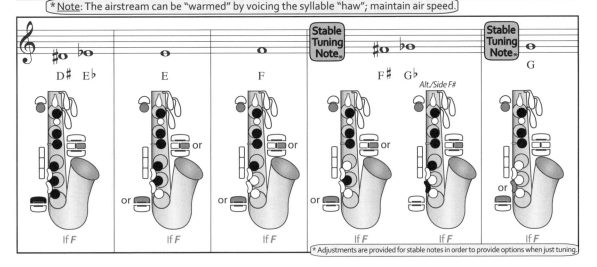

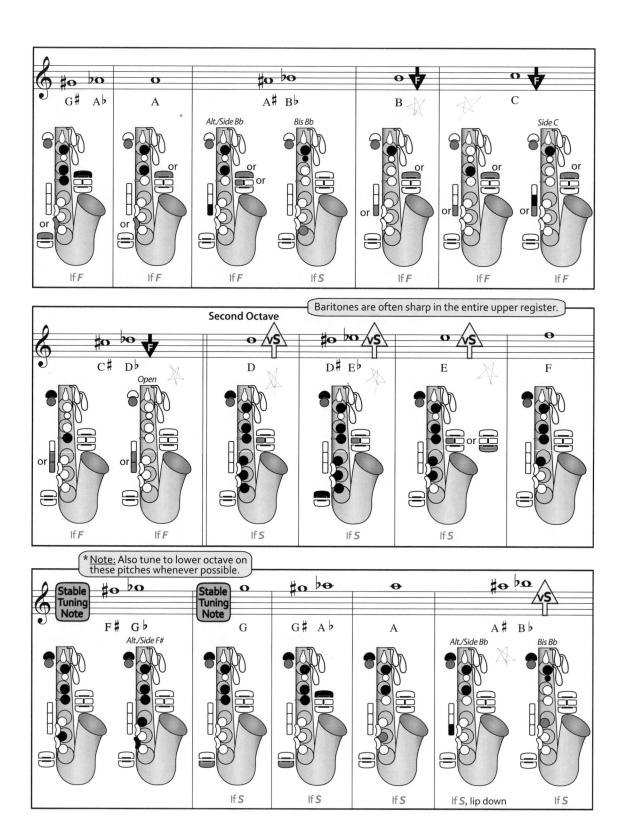

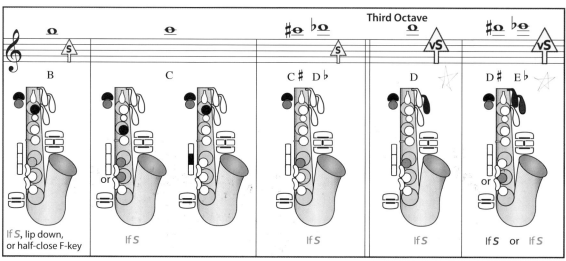

Third Octave

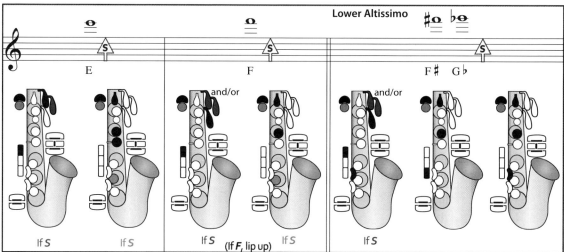

Lower Altissimo

**General Note:**   The saxophone will play *sharper* in pitch as one plays *softer*.

The saxophone will play *flatter* in pitch as one plays *louder*.

To ▼ pitch, one can *close* selected tone holes and keys to a regular fingering.

To ⑤ pitch, one can *open* selected tone holes and keys to a regular fingering.

! CAUTION !

Every instrument, even identical models, can have varying pitch tendencies. Learn the pitch of your instrument and advance your skills to *voice / place / lip* every note in tune. Alternate fingerings are simply one option.

**If *consistently* sharp in pitch:**
1. Is embouchure too tight?
2. Is reed strength too hard; biting?
3. Is mouthpiece pushed in too far?

**If *consistently* flat in pitch:**
1. Is embouchure too loose?
2. Is reed strength too soft?
3. Is mouthpiece pulled out too far?

**Figure 6.5.** Bassoon Fingering Chart

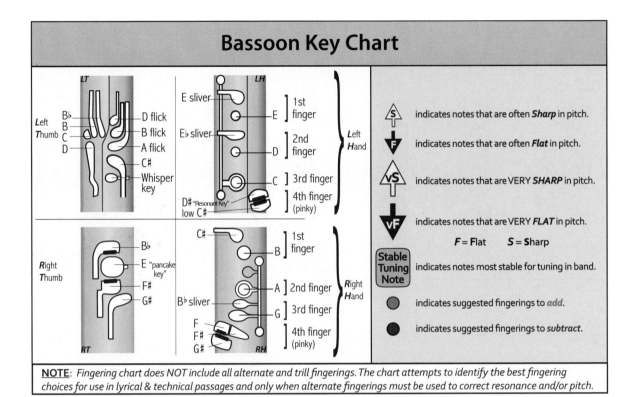

# Bassoon Key Chart

**NOTE**: _Fingering chart does NOT include all alternate and trill fingerings. The chart attempts to identify the best fingering choices for use in lyrical & technical passages and only when alternate fingerings must be used to correct resonance and/or pitch._

**General Note:** The bassoon will play **sharper** in pitch as one plays **softer**.

The bassoon will play **flatter** in pitch as one plays **louder**.

To ▼ pitch, one can **close** selected tone holes and keys to a regular fingering.

To ▲ pitch, one can **open** selected tone holes and keys to a regular fingering.

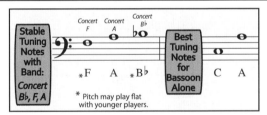

**To correct sharpness in pitch**:
1. Relax lips and compression on reed; lips still puckered, but with less firmness.
2. Open up the inside of mouth to reduce _biting_; (vowel = **aw**)

**To correct flatness in pitch**: (make sure bocal and reed is pushed in all the way), then:
1. Use a faster and more focused air; maintain air support and aim air forward and higher in mouth (vowel = **ee**)
2. Firm the lips; use a smaller lip opening and press lip corners _in_ to sides of reed.
3. Take more reed in mouth; more lips in contact with reed.

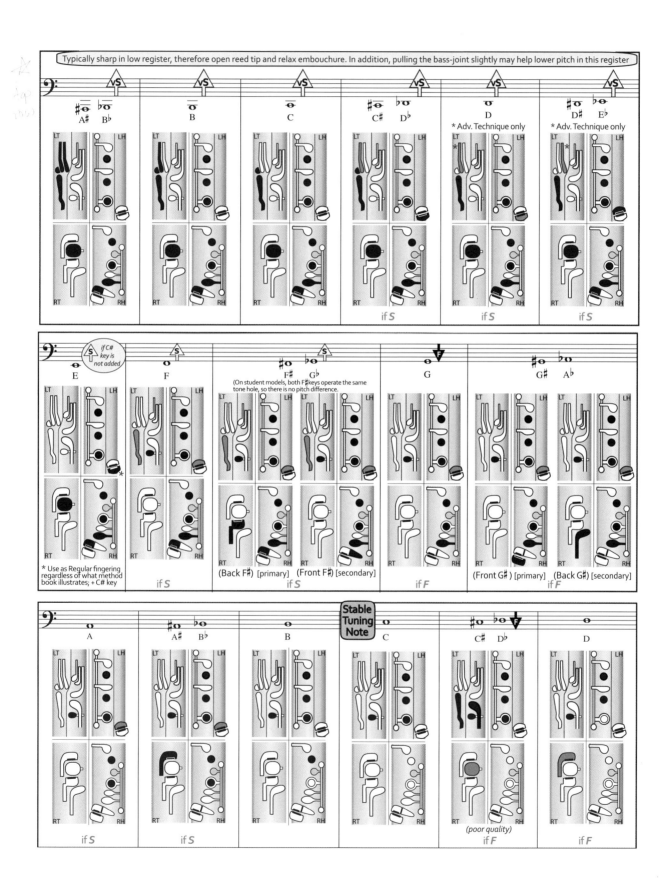

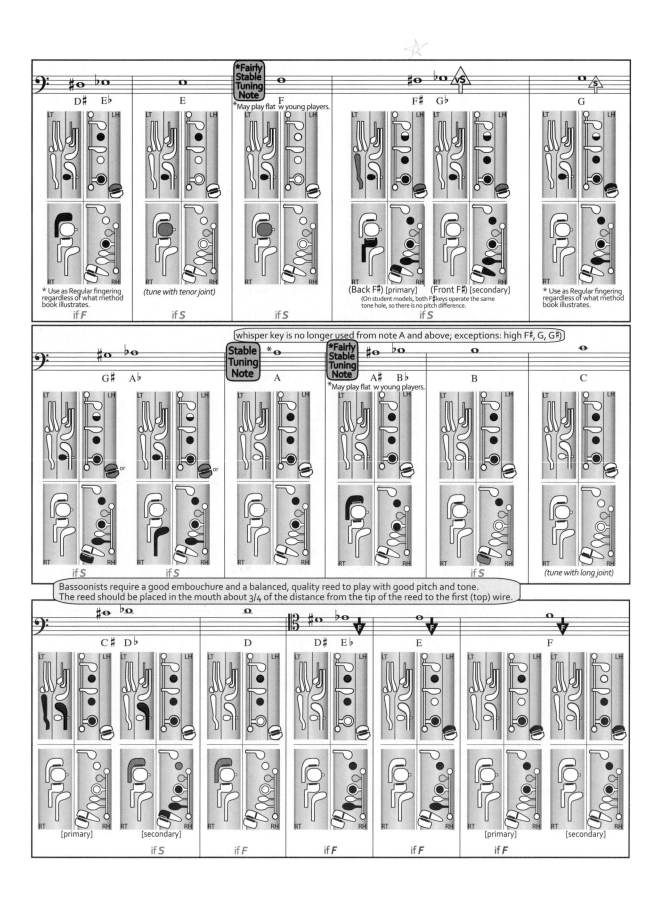

whisper key is used again for high F#, G, G#

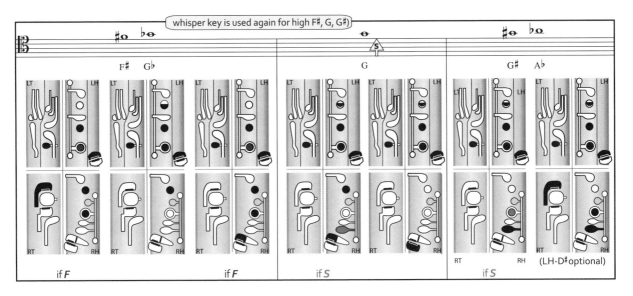

| F# | Gb | | G | | G# | Ab |
|---|---|---|---|---|---|---|
| if *F* | if *F* | | if *S* | | if *S* | |

(LH-D# optional)

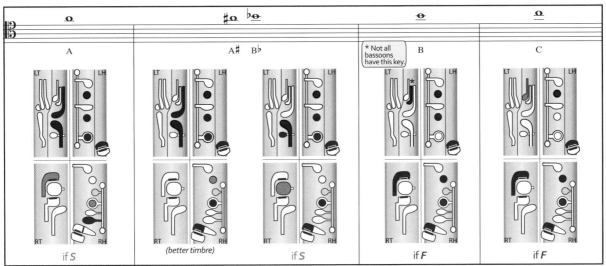

| A | A# | Bb | B | C |
|---|---|---|---|---|
| if *S* | *(better timbre)* | if *S* | if *F* | if *F* |

\* Not all bassoons have this key.

! CAUTION !

Every instrument, even identical models, can have varying pitch tendencies. Learn the pitch of your instrument and advance your skills to *voice / place / lip* every note in tune. Use alternate fingerings only when necessary!

If *consistently* sharp in pitch:
1. Is embouchure too tight?
2. Is reed strength too hard?
3. Taking too much reed in mouth?
4. Is bocal length too short?

If *consistently* flat in pitch:
1. Is embouchure too loose?
2. Is reed strength too soft?
3. Taking too little reed in mouth?
4. Is bocal length too long?

**Figure 6.6.** Horn Fingering Chart

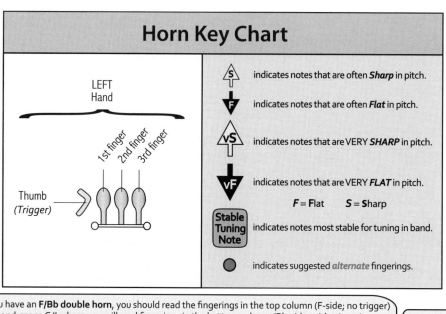

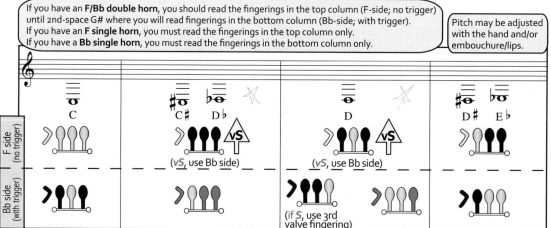

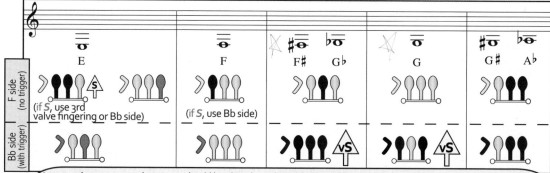

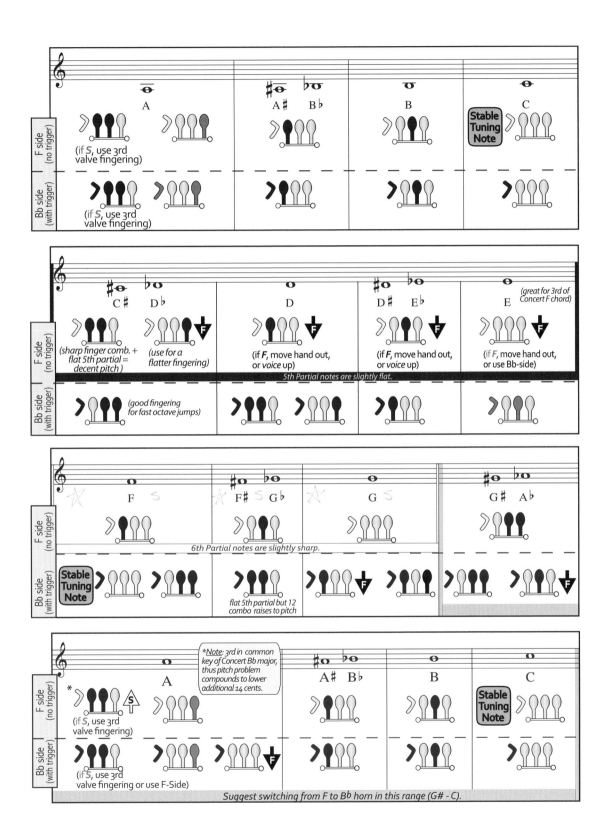

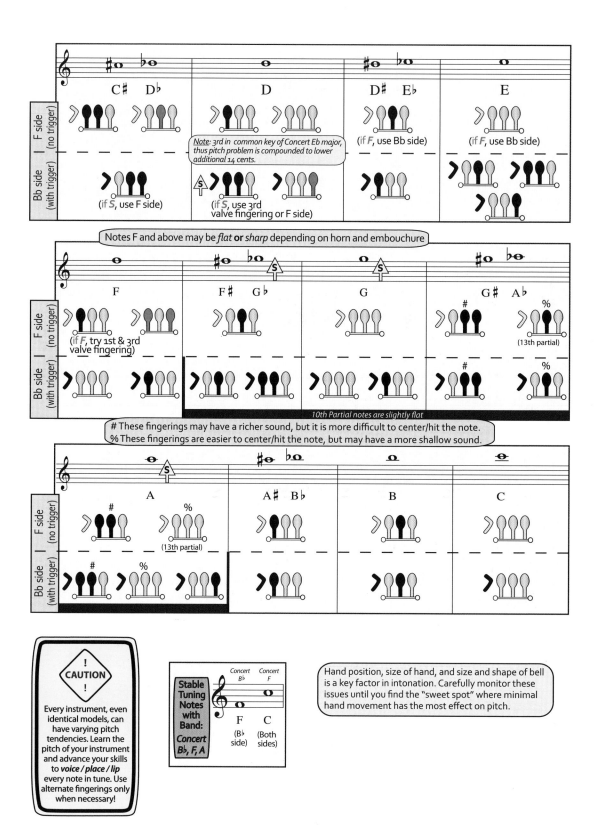

**Figure 6.7.** Trumpet Fingering Chart

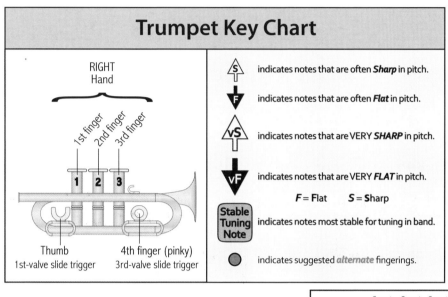

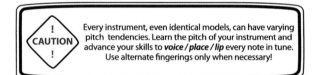

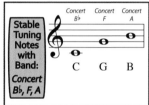

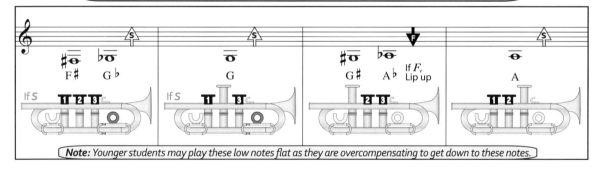

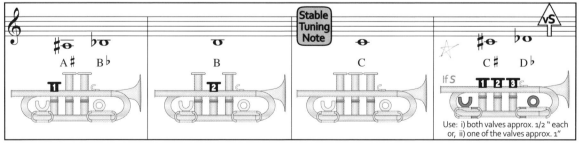

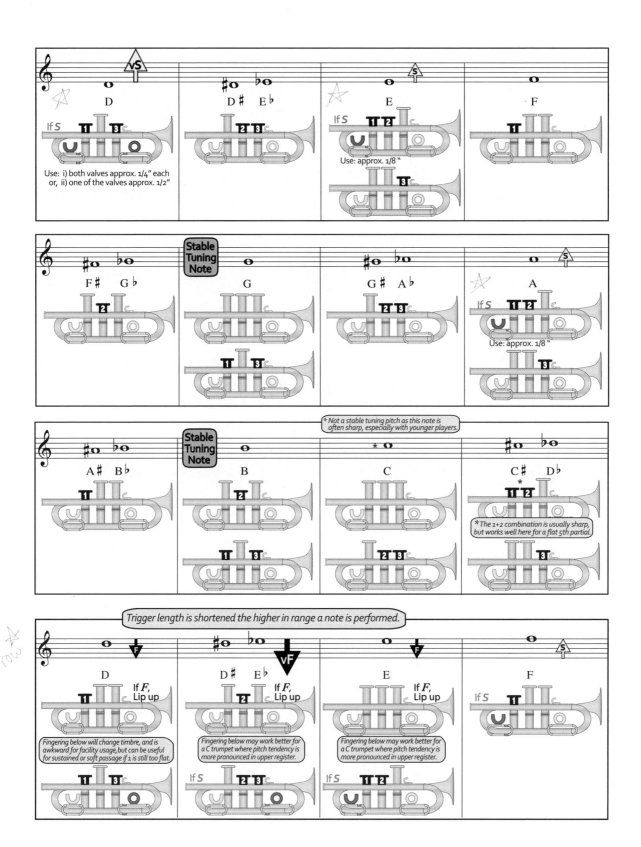

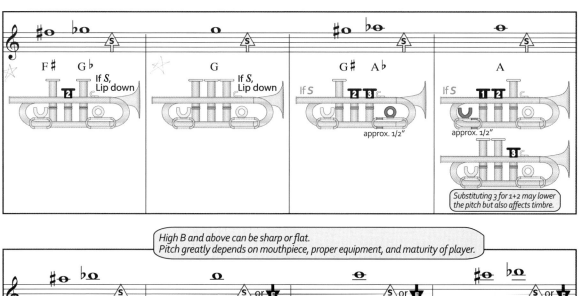

High B and above can be sharp or flat.
Pitch greatly depends on mouthpiece, proper equipment, and maturity of player.

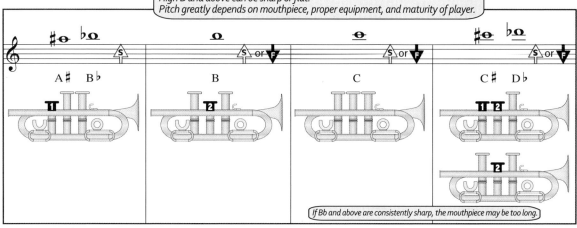

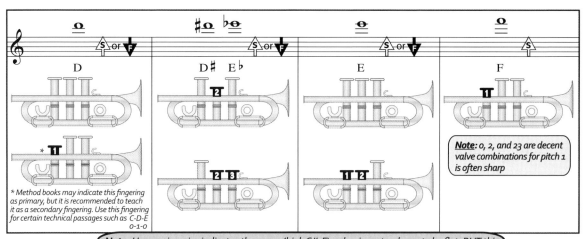

**Figure 6.8.** Trombone Fingering Chart

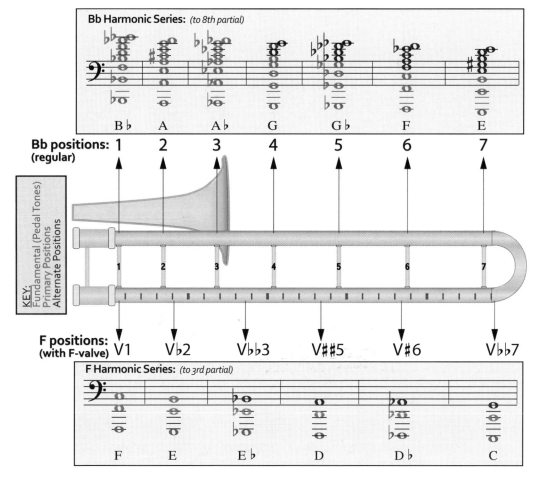

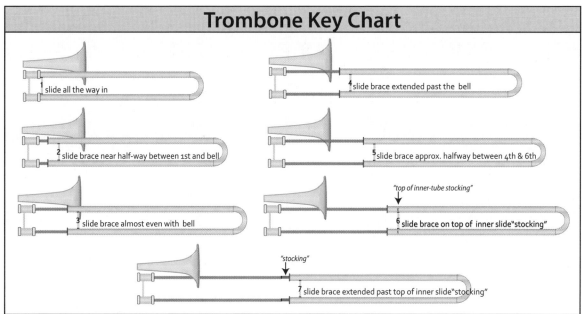

**NOTE:** Resources and teachers vary in how they notate slide placement in relationship to the position. For clarity, this chart uses ♯ = Shorten and ♭ = Lengthen.

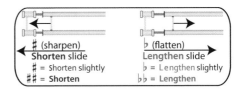

♯ (sharpen)  
**Shorten** slide  
♯ = Shorten slightly  
♯♯ = **Shorten**

♭ (flatten)  
Lengthen slide  
♭ = Lengthen slightly  
♭♭ = Lengthen

*Traditional fingering chart ascending chromatically.*

| B | C | C♯ D♭ | D | D♯ E♭ | E | F | F♯ G♭ |
|---|---|-------|---|-------|---|---|-------|
| * also extend F-attachment tuning slide | | | | | 7 | 6 | 5 |
| V♭♭7* | V♭♭7 | V♯6 | V♯♯5 | V♭♭3 | V♭2 | V1 | |

| G | G♯ A♭ | A | A♯ B♭ (Stable Tuning Note) | B | C | C♯ D♭ |
|---|-------|---|--------------------------|---|---|-------|
| 4 | 3 | 2 | 1 | 7 | 6 | 5 |
| V♭♭7 | V♯6 | V♯♯5 | V♭♭3 | V♭2 | V♭1 | |

| D | D♯ E♭ | E | F (*Fairly Stable Tuning Note) | F♯ G♭ | G | G♯ A♭ |
|---|-------|---|-------------------------------|-------|---|-------|
| 4 | 3 | 2 / 7 | * 3rd partial can be slightly sharp  1 / 6 | 5 | 4 | 3 / ♯7 |

| A (Stable Tuning Note) | A♯ B♭ | B | C | C♯ D♭ | D | D♯ E♭ | E |
|------------------------|-------|---|---|-------|---|-------|---|
| 2 / ♯6 | 1 / ♯5 | ♯4 / ♭7 | ♯3 / ♭6 | ♯2 / ♭5 | 1 / ♭4 | ♭3 / ♯♯6 | ♭2 / ♯♯5 |

| F | F♯ G♭ | G | G♯ A♭ | A | A♯ B♭ | B | C |
|---|-------|---|-------|---|-------|---|---|
| ♭1 / ♯♯4 | ♯♯3 / 5 | ♯♯2 / 4 | 3 / ♭5 | 2 / ♭4 | 1 / ♭3 | ♭2 / ♯4 | ♭1 / ♯3 |

| Trombone F-Attachment Tuning | | |
|---|---|---|
| • The main tuning slide should be pulled out slightly (1/2"-1") before you start to tune. | | • Depress the F-attachment trigger when moving the F-Main Slide. |
| **STEP 1** | Play Concert B♭ (or Concert F for younger players) — 1 / (1)   Tune with main tuning slide:  If flat, push in.  If sharp, pull out. | ...then match your tuned F to the F an octave lower with F-trigger depressed. *Tip*: Younger players should tune only to high F until embouchure is more developed.   1   V1 |
| **STEP 2** | Play Concert F with the *F-attachment* — V1 | *Tip*: It is easier to hear the pitch approached from below. This also assists players to hear various positions in tune. |

**Figure 6.9.** Euphonium Fingering Chart

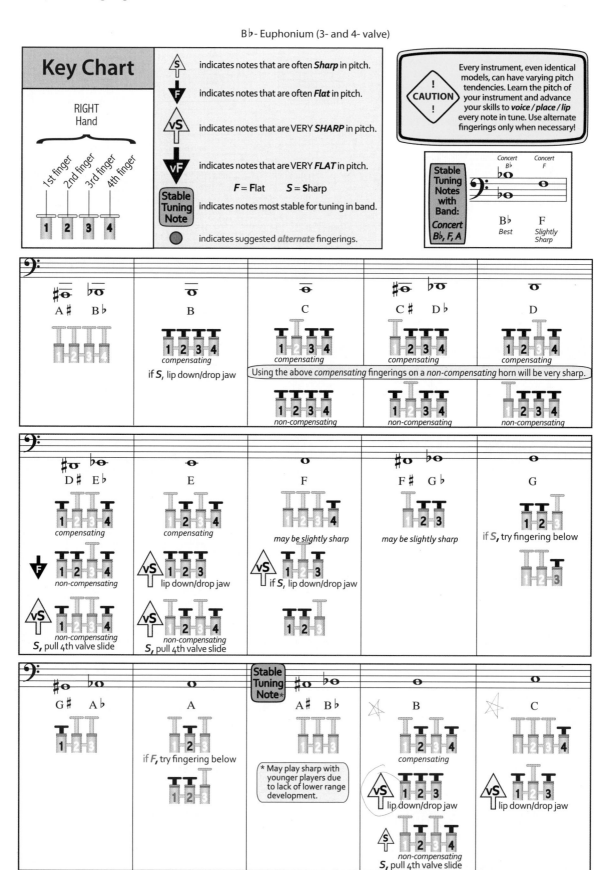

B♭ - Euphonium (3- and 4- valve)

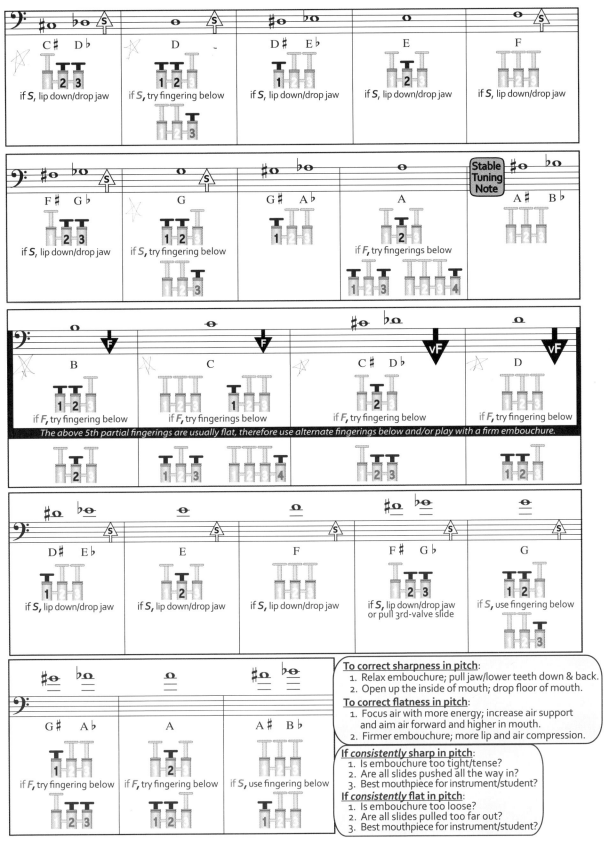

To correct sharpness in pitch:
1. Relax embouchure; pull jaw/lower teeth down & back.
2. Open up the inside of mouth; drop floor of mouth.

To correct flatness in pitch:
1. Focus air with more energy; increase air support and aim air forward and higher in mouth.
2. Firmer embouchure; more lip and air compression.

If *consistently* sharp in pitch:
1. Is embouchure too tight/tense?
2. Are all slides pushed all the way in?
3. Best mouthpiece for instrument/student?

If *consistently* flat in pitch:
1. Is embouchure too loose?
2. Are all slides pulled too far out?
3. Best mouthpiece for instrument/student?

**Figure 6.10.** Tuba Fingering Chart

BB♭- Tuba (3- and 4- valve)

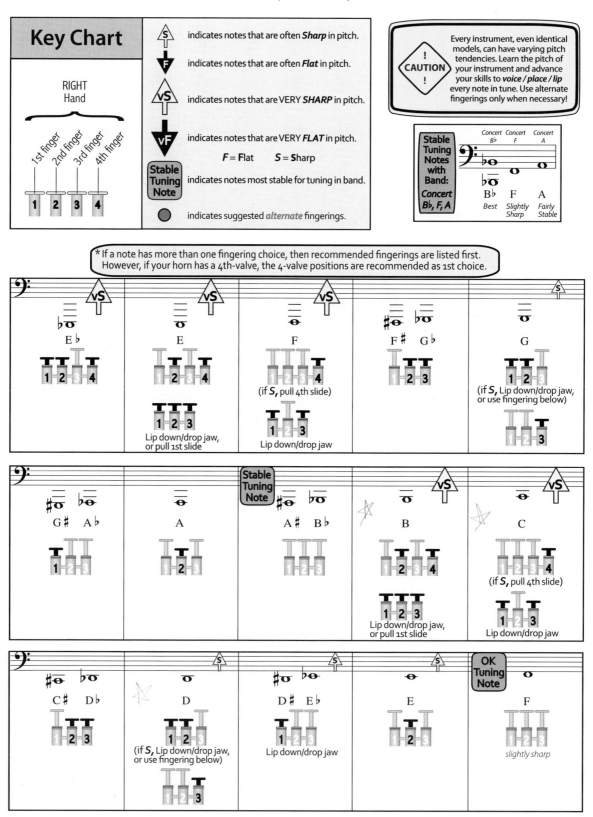

BB♭- Tuba (3- and 4- valve)

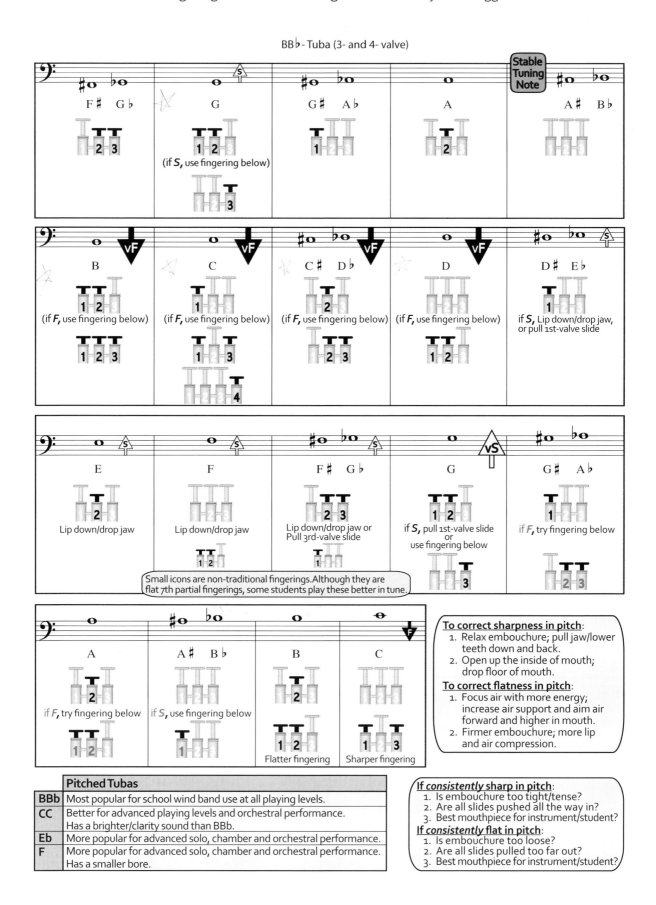

| Pitched Tubas | |
|---|---|
| BBb | Most popular for school wind band use at all playing levels. |
| CC | Better for advanced playing levels and orchestral performance. Has a brighter/clarity sound than BBb. |
| Eb | More popular for advanced solo, chamber and orchestral performance. |
| F | More popular for advanced solo, chamber and orchestral performance. Has a smaller bore. |

**To correct sharpness in pitch:**
1. Relax embouchure; pull jaw/lower teeth down and back.
2. Open up the inside of mouth; drop floor of mouth.

**To correct flatness in pitch:**
1. Focus air with more energy; increase air support and aim air forward and higher in mouth.
2. Firmer embouchure; more lip and air compression.

**If _consistently_ sharp in pitch:**
1. Is embouchure too tight/tense?
2. Are all slides pushed all the way in?
3. Best mouthpiece for instrument/student?

**If _consistently_ flat in pitch:**
1. Is embouchure too loose?
2. Are all slides pulled too far out?
3. Best mouthpiece for instrument/student?

## BRASS HARMONIC SERIES CHARTS

**Figure 6.11.** Horn Harmonic Series

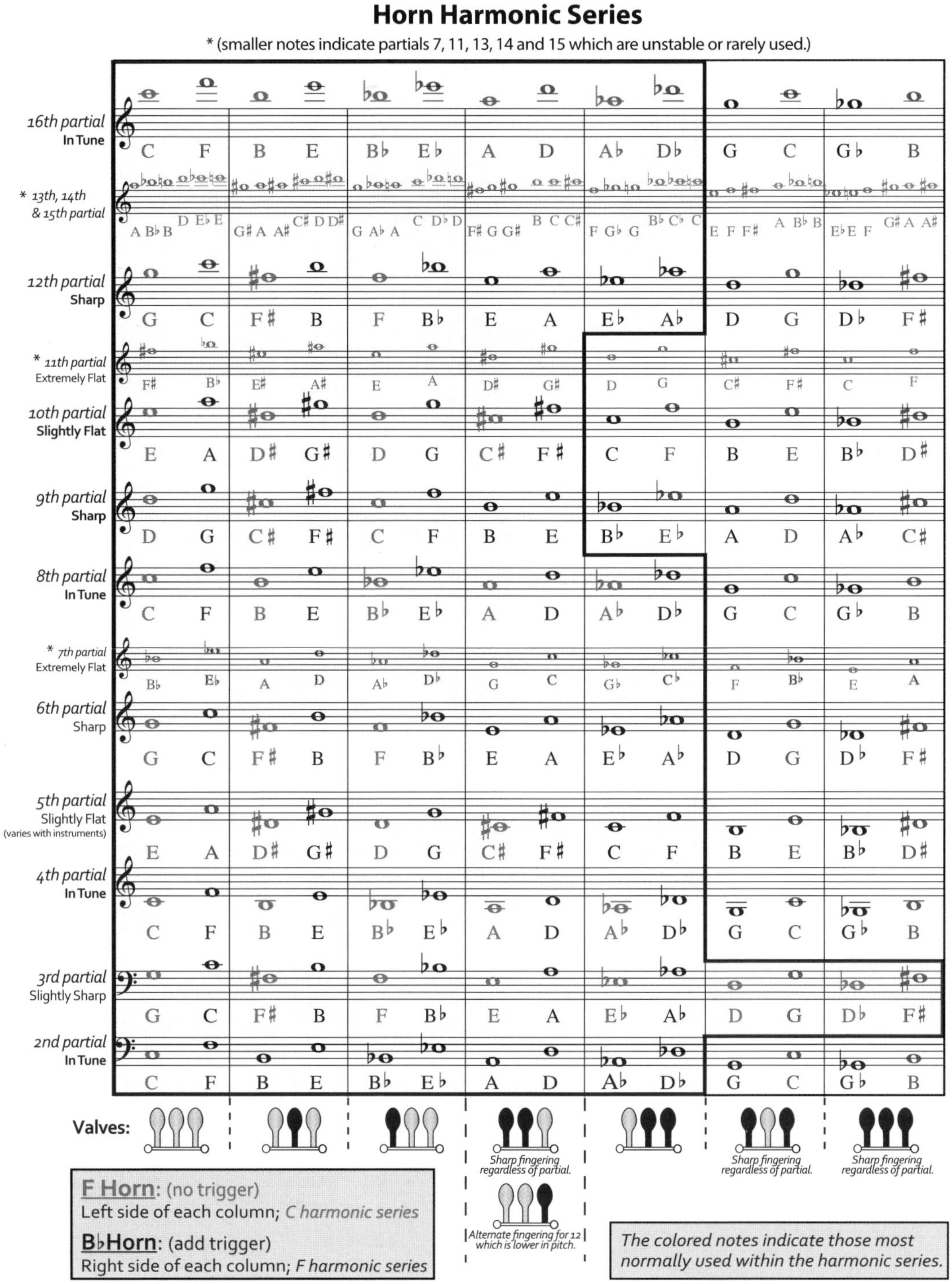
Horn Harmonic Series
* (smaller notes indicate partials 7, 11, 13, 14 and 15 which are unstable or rarely used.)
16th partial In Tune
C F B E B♭ E♭ A D A♭ D♭ G C G♭ B
* 13th, 14th & 15th partial
A B♭ B D E♭ E G♯ A A♯ C♯ D D♯ G A♭ A C D♭ D F♯ G G♯ B C C♯ F G♭ G B♭ C♭ C E F F♯ A B♭ B E♭ E F G♯ A A♯
12th partial Sharp
G C F♯ B F B♭ E A E♭ A♭ D G D♭ F♯
* 11th partial Extremely Flat
F♯ B♭ E♯ A♯ E A D♯ G♯ D G C♯ F♯ C F
10th partial Slightly Flat
E A D♯ G♯ D G C♯ F♯ C F B E B♭ D♯
9th partial Sharp
D G C♯ F♯ C F B E B♭ E♭ A D A♭ C♯
8th partial In Tune
C F B E B♭ E♭ A D A♭ D♭ G C G♭ B
* 7th partial Extremely Flat
B♭ E♭ A D A♭ D♭ G C G♭ C♭ F B♭ E A
6th partial Sharp
G C F♯ B F B♭ E A E♭ A♭ D G D♭ F♯
5th partial Slightly Flat (varies with instruments)
E A D♯ G♯ D G C♯ F♯ C F B E B♭ D♯
4th partial In Tune
C F B E B♭ E♭ A D A♭ D♭ G C G♭ B
3rd partial Slightly Sharp
G C F♯ B F B♭ E A E♭ A♭ D G D♭ F♯
2nd partial In Tune
C F B E B♭ E♭ A D A♭ D♭ G C G♭ B
Valves:
Sharp fingering regardless of partial.
Sharp fingering regardless of partial.
Sharp fingering regardless of partial.
Alternate fingering for 12 which is lower in pitch.
F Horn: (no trigger)
Left side of each column; C harmonic series
B♭ Horn: (add trigger)
Right side of each column; F harmonic series
The colored notes indicate those most normally used within the harmonic series.

**Figure 6.12.** Trumpet Harmonic Series

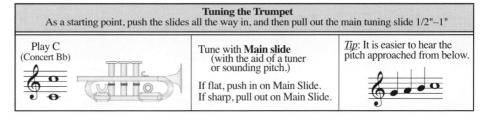

**Figure 6.13.** Trombone Harmonic Series

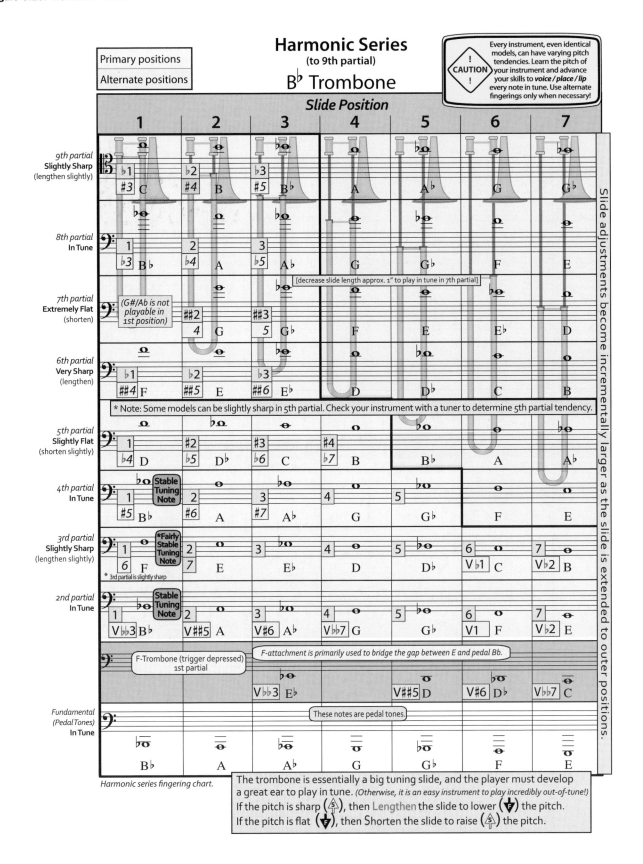

Harmonic series fingering chart.

The trombone is essentially a big tuning slide, and the player must develop a great ear to play in tune. *(Otherwise, it is an easy instrument to play incredibly out-of-tune!)*
If the pitch is sharp, then Lengthen the slide to lower the pitch.
If the pitch is flat, then Shorten the slide to raise the pitch.

**Figure 6.14.** Euphonium Harmonic Series

**Euphonium Harmonic Series**
* (shaded notes indicates a partial which is unstable or rarely used.)
*Note: Chart indicates general pitch tendencies of the harmonic series; degree of tendency may vary by instrument.*

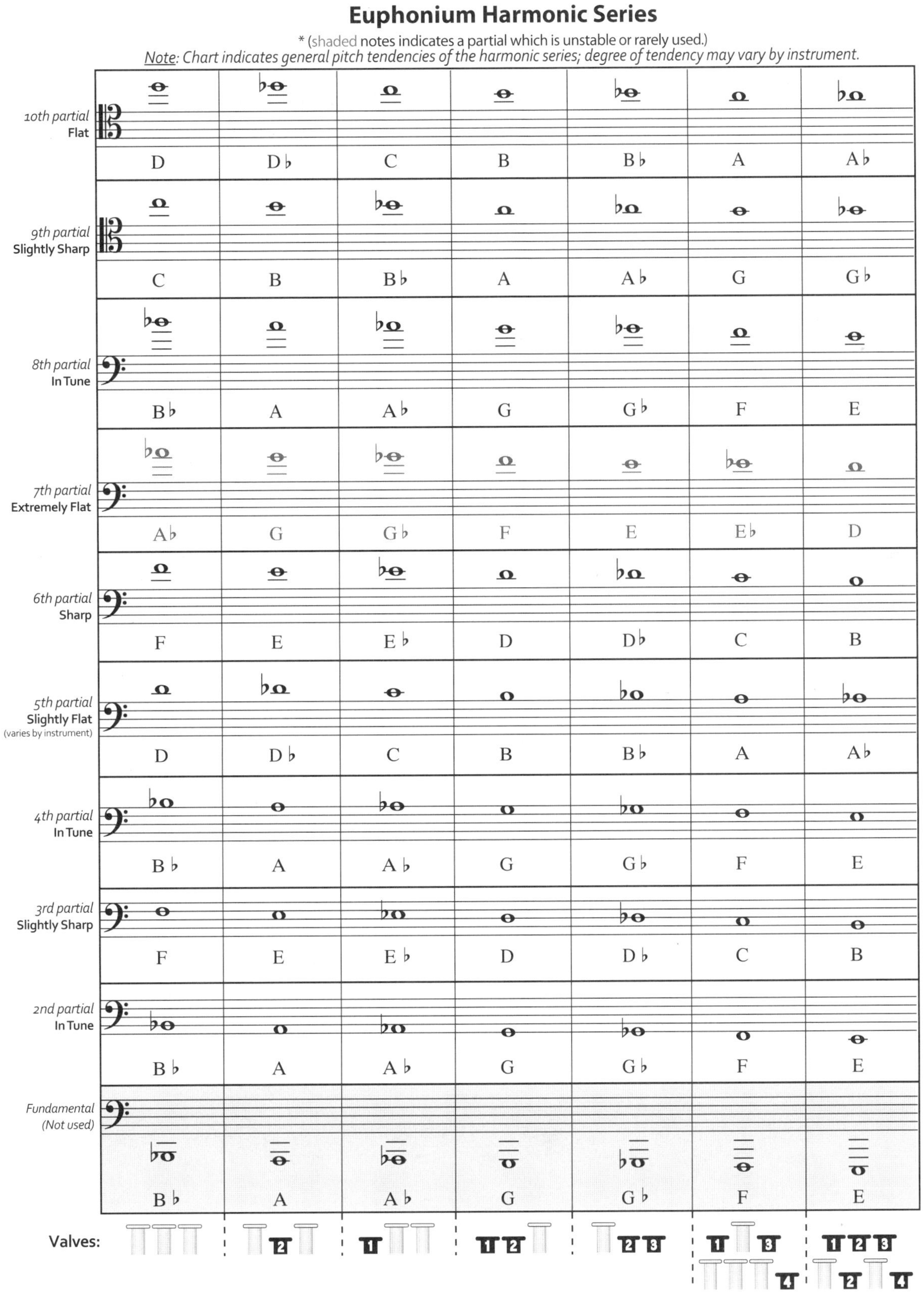

**Figure 6.15.** Tuba Harmonic Series

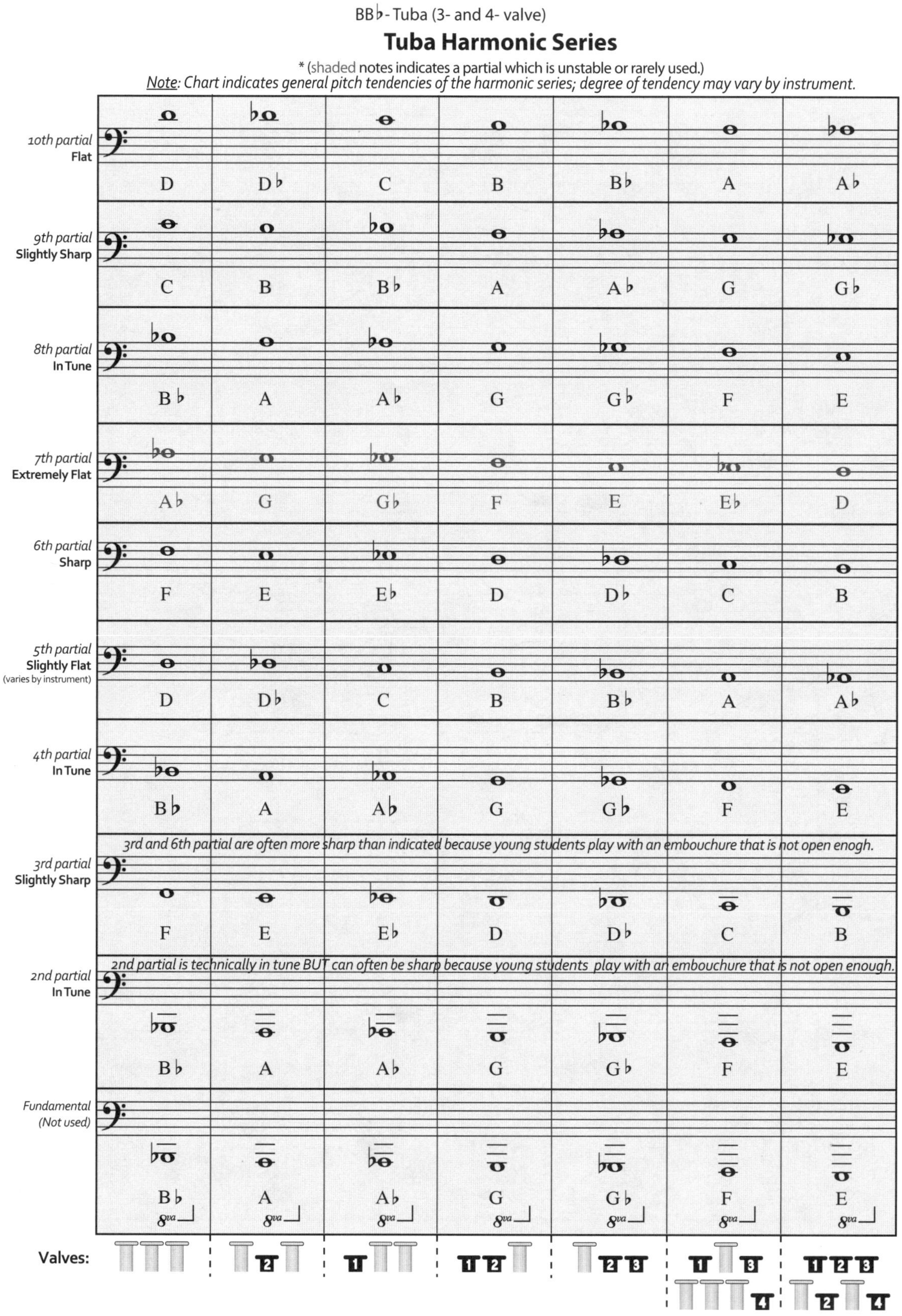

BB♭- Tuba (3- and 4- valve)
## Tuba Harmonic Series
*(shaded notes indicates a partial which is unstable or rarely used.)
_Note: Chart indicates general pitch tendencies of the harmonic series; degree of tendency may vary by instrument._

| | | | | | | | |
|---|---|---|---|---|---|---|---|
| **10th partial** Flat | D | D♭ | C | B | B♭ | A | A♭ |
| **9th partial** Slightly Sharp | C | B | B♭ | A | A♭ | G | G♭ |
| **8th partial** In Tune | B♭ | A | A♭ | G | G♭ | F | E |
| **7th partial** Extremely Flat | A♭ | G | G♭ | F | E | E♭ | D |
| **6th partial** Sharp | F | E | E♭ | D | D♭ | C | B |
| **5th partial** Slightly Flat (varies by instrument) | D | D♭ | C | B | B♭ | A | A♭ |
| **4th partial** In Tune | B♭ | A | A♭ | G | G♭ | F | E |
| **3rd partial** Slightly Sharp | F | E | E♭ | D | D♭ | C | B |
| **2nd partial** In Tune | B♭ | A | A♭ | G | G♭ | F | E |
| **Fundamental** (Not used) | B♭ | A | A♭ | G | G♭ | F | E |

_3rd and 6th partial are often more sharp than indicated because young students play with an embouchure that is not open enogh._

_2nd partial is technically in tune BUT can often be sharp because young students play with an embouchure that is not open enough._

(8va on Fundamental row)

Valves:  open | 2 | 1 | 1 2 | 2 3 | 1 3 / 4 | 1 2 3 / 1 2 4

# Blank Intonation Charts by Instrument

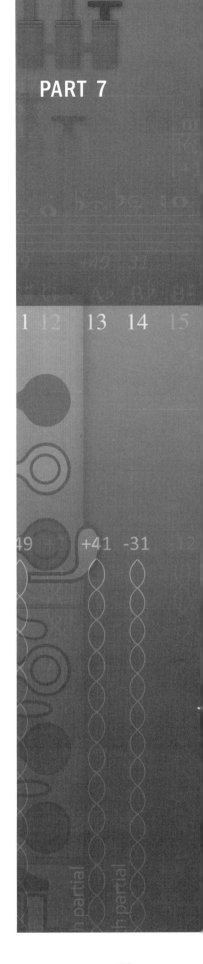

# PART 7

The following pages include blank intonation charts for each instrument in order for a student to *map* the pitch tendencies of their instrument.

**Instructions:**

1. Properly warm up your instrument and then tune to A = 440.

2. Sustain a written note on your instrument 2 or 3 times in a row while a friend watches the tuner:

   a. If the average of the notes is in tune, or it displays as only a few cents sharp or flat, don't mark anything on the chart.

   b. If the average of the notes is flat (more than 5 cents), write the number of cents flat; i.e. −12

   c. If the average of the notes is sharp (more than 5 cents), write the number of cents sharp; i.e. +12

3. Repeat step #2 for every note within the range of your instrument.

4. When you have completed the Check Sheet, go back to the notes that were MOST out of tune and learn solutions to play them in tune by improving tone, correcting your embouchure, using alternate fingerings, etc.

If you have difficulty getting any particular notes in tune, please read Part 8: Factors Affecting Pitch and Table 8.1.

When you revisit your Intonation Check-Sheet, ALWAYS USE YOUR EARS FIRST BEFORE YOUR EYES!

Hear every note before you play it, and then *place* the note with good tone and pitch using proper air and embouchure.

**Figure 7.1.** Flute Intonation Chart Template

## FLUTE INTONATION CHECK-SHEET

Name: _____

Headjoint: _____

Notes: _____

**Instructions:**

1. Properly warm up your instrument and then tune to A = 440.
2. Sustain a written note on your instrument 2 or 3 times in a row while a friend watches the tuner:
   a. If the average of the notes is in tune, or it displays as only a few cents sharp or flat, don't mark anything.
   b. If the average of the notes is flat (more than 5 cents), write the number of cents flat; ie. -12
   c. If the average of the notes is sharp (more than 5 cents), write the number of cents sharp; ie. +12
3. Repeat step #2 for every note within the range of your instrument.
4. When you have completed the Check Sheet, go back to the notes that were MOST out of tune and learn solutions to play them in tune by improving tone, firming or relaxing your embouchure, using alternate fingerings, etc. If you have difficulty getting any particular notes in tune, please read the chapter *Factors Affecting Pitch*. When you revisit your Intonation Check-Sheet, ALWAYS USE YOUR **EARS** FIRST BEFORE YOUR **EYES**!

| | B | C | C♯ D♭ | D | D♯ E♭ | E | F | F♯ G♭ | G | G♯ A♭ | A | A♯ B♭ | B |
|---|---|---|---|---|---|---|---|---|---|---|---|---|---|
| **Number of cents flat (-) or sharp (+):** -  + | | | | | | | | | | | | | |
| **Solutions:** | | | | | | | | | | | | | |

| | C | C♯ D♭ | D | D♯ E♭ | E | F | F♯ G♭ | G | G♯ A♭ | A | A♯ B♭ | B | C |
|---|---|---|---|---|---|---|---|---|---|---|---|---|---|---|
| **Number of cents flat (-) or sharp (+):** -  + | | | | | | | | | | | | | | |
| **Solutions:** | | | | | | | | | | | | | | |

| | C♯ D♭ | D | D♯ E♭ | E | F | F♯ G♭ | G | G♯ A♭ | A | A♯ B♭ | B | C |
|---|---|---|---|---|---|---|---|---|---|---|---|---|---|
| **Number of cents flat (-) or sharp (+):** -  + | | | | | | | | | | | | | |
| **Solutions:** | | | | | | | | | | | | | |

**Figure 7.2.**  Oboe Intonation Chart Template

## OBOE INTONATION CHECK-SHEET

**Instructions:**

1. Properly warm up your instrument and then tune to A = 440.
2. Sustain a written note on your instrument 2 or 3 times in a row while a friend watches the tuner:
   a. If the average of the notes is in tune, or it displays as only a few cents sharp or flat, don't mark anything.
   b. If the average of the notes is flat (more than 5 cents), write the number of cents flat; ie. -12
   c. If the average of the notes is sharp (more than 5 cents), write the number of cents sharp; ie. +12
3. Repeat step #2 for every note within the range of your instrument.
4. When you have completed the Check Sheet, go back to the notes that were MOST out of tune and learn solutions to play them in tune by improving tone, firming or relaxing your embouchure, using alternate fingerings, etc. If you have difficulty getting any particular notes in tune, please read the chapter *Factors Affecting Pitch*. When you revisit your Intonation Check-Sheet, ALWAYS USE YOUR **EARS** FIRST BEFORE YOUR **EYES**!

Name: _____
Reed: _____
Notes: _____

| | A♯ B♭ | B | C | C♯ D♭ | D | D♯ E♭ | E | F | F♯ G♭ | G | G♯ A♭ |
|---|---|---|---|---|---|---|---|---|---|---|---|
| **Number of cents flat (-) or sharp (+):** | - + | - + | - + | - + | - + | - + | - + | - + | - + | - + | - + |
| **Solutions:** | | | | | | | | | | | |

| | A | A♯ B♭ | B | C | C♯ D♭ | D | D♯ E♭ | E | F | F♯ G♭ | G |
|---|---|---|---|---|---|---|---|---|---|---|---|
| **Number of cents flat (-) or sharp (+):** | - + | - + | - + | - + | - + | - + | - + | - + | - + | - + | - + |
| **Solutions:** | | | | | | | | | | | |

| | G♯ A♭ | A | A♯ B♭ | B | C | C♯ D♭ | D | D♯ E♭ | E | F | F♯ G♭ |
|---|---|---|---|---|---|---|---|---|---|---|---|
| **Number of cents flat (-) or sharp (+):** | - + | - + | - + | - + | - + | - + | - + | - + | - + | - + | - + |
| **Solutions:** | | | | | | | | | | | |

**Figure 7.3.** Clarinet Intonation Chart Template

## CLARINET INTONATION CHECK-SHEET

**Instructions:**

1. Properly warm up your instrument and then tune to A = 440.
2. Sustain a written note on your instrument 2 or 3 times in a row while a friend watches the tuner:
   a. If the average of the notes is in tune, or it displays as only a few cents sharp or flat, don't mark anything.
   b. If the average of the notes is flat (more than 5 cents), write the number of cents flat; ie. -12
   c. If the average of the notes is sharp (more than 5 cents), write the number of cents sharp; ie. +12
3. Repeat step #2 for every note within the range of your instrument.
4. When you have completed the Check Sheet, go back to the notes that were MOST out of tune and learn solutions to play them in tune by improving tone, firming or relaxing your embouchure, using alternate fingerings, etc. If you have difficulty getting any particular notes in tune, please read the chapter *Factors Affecting Pitch.* When you revisit your Intonation Check-Sheet, ALWAYS USE YOUR **EARS** FIRST BEFORE YOUR **EYES!**

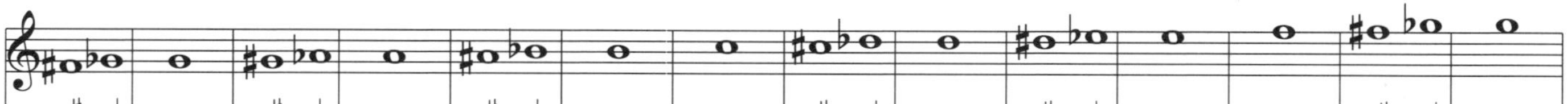

Name: _____
Mouthpiece: _____
Reed: _____
Notes: _____

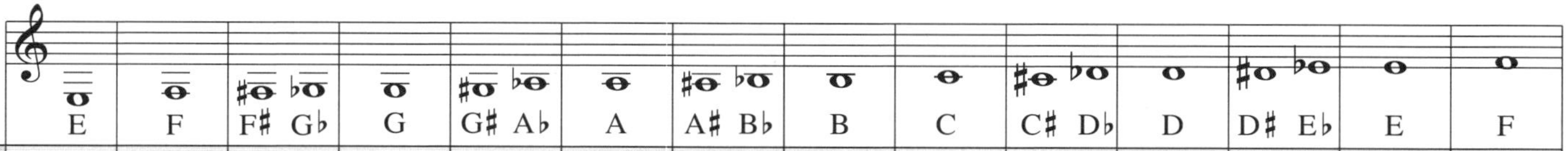

| | E | F | F# Gb | G | G# Ab | A | A# Bb | B | C | C# Db | D | D# Eb | E | F |
|---|---|---|---|---|---|---|---|---|---|---|---|---|---|---|
| **Number of cents flat (-) or sharp (+):** | - + | - + | - + | - + | - + | - + | - + | - + | - + | - + | - + | - + | - + | - + |
| **Solutions:** | | | | | | | | | | | | | | |

| | F# Gb | G | G# Ab | A | A# Bb | B | C | C# Db | D | D# Eb | E | F | F# Gb | G |
|---|---|---|---|---|---|---|---|---|---|---|---|---|---|---|
| **Number of cents flat (-) or sharp (+):** | - + | - + | - + | - + | - + | - + | - + | - + | - + | - + | - + | - + | - + | - + |
| **Solutions:** | | | | | | | | | | | | | | |

| | G# Ab | A | A# Bb | B | C | C# Db | D | D# Eb | E | F | F# Gb | G | G# Ab | A |
|---|---|---|---|---|---|---|---|---|---|---|---|---|---|---|
| **Number of cents flat (-) or sharp (+):** | - + | - + | - + | - + | - + | - + | - + | - + | - + | - + | - + | - + | - + | - + |
| **Solutions:** | | | | | | | | | | | | | | |

**Figure 7.4.** Saxophone Intonation Chart Template

## SAXOPHONE INTONATION CHECK-SHEET

**Instructions:**

1. Properly warm up your instrument and then tune to A = 440.
2. Sustain a written note on your instrument 2 or 3 times in a row while a friend watches the tuner:
   a. If the average of the notes is in tune, or it displays as only a few cents sharp or flat, don't mark anything.
   b. If the average of the notes is flat (more than 5 cents), write the number of cents flat; ie. -12
   c. If the average of the notes is sharp (more than 5 cents), write the number of cents sharp; ie. +12
3. Repeat step #2 for every note within the range of your instrument.
4. When you have completed the Check Sheet, go back to the notes that were MOST out of tune and learn solutions to play them in tune by improving tone, firming or relaxing your embouchure, using alternate fingerings, etc.
   If you have difficulty getting any particular notes in tune, please read the chapter *Factors Affecting Pitch.*
   When you revisit your Intonation Check-Sheet, ALWAYS USE YOUR **EARS** FIRST BEFORE YOUR EYES!

**Name:** __________

**Mouthpiece:** __________

**Reed:** __________

**Notes:**

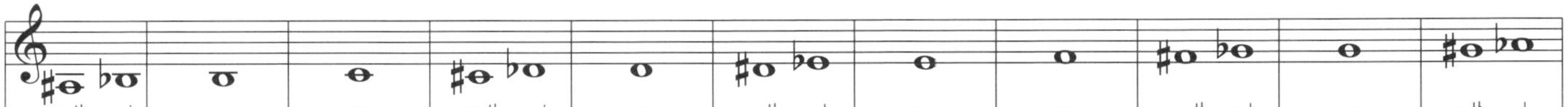

| | | | | | | | | | | | |
|---|---|---|---|---|---|---|---|---|---|---|---|
| | A♯ B♭ | B | C | C♯ D♭ | D | D♯ E♭ | E | F | F♯ G♭ | G | G♯ A♭ |
| **Number of cents flat (-) or sharp (+):** | - + | - + | - + | - + | - + | - + | - + | - + | - + | - + | - + |
| ***Solutions:*** | | | | | | | | | | | |

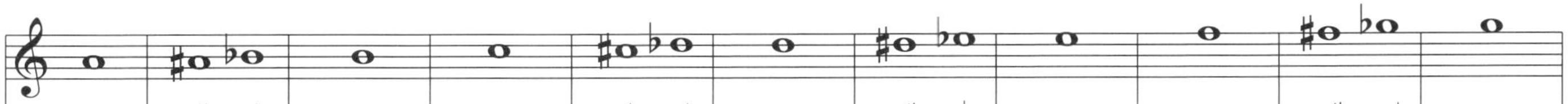

| | | | | | | | | | | | |
|---|---|---|---|---|---|---|---|---|---|---|---|
| | A | A♯ B♭ | B | C | C♯ D♭ | D | D♯ E♭ | E | F | F♯ G♭ | G |
| **Number of cents flat (-) or sharp (+):** | - + | - + | - + | - + | - + | - + | - + | - + | - + | - + | - + |
| ***Solutions:*** | | | | | | | | | | | |

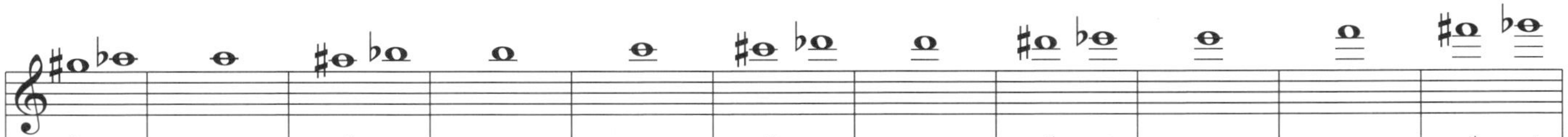

| | | | | | | | | | | | |
|---|---|---|---|---|---|---|---|---|---|---|---|
| | G♯ A♭ | A | A♯ B♭ | B | C | C♯ D♭ | D | D♯ E♭ | E | F | F♯ G♭ |
| **Number of cents flat (-) or sharp (+):** | - + | - + | - + | - + | - + | - + | - + | - + | - + | - + | - + |
| ***Solutions:*** | | | | | | | | | | | |

**Figure 7.5.** Bassoon Intonation Chart Template

## BASSOON INTONATION CHECK-SHEET

Name: _____

Bocal: _____

Reed: _____

Notes: _____

### Instructions:

1. Properly warm up your instrument and then tune to A = 440.
2. Sustain a written note on your instrument 2 or 3 times in a row while a friend watches the tuner:
   a. If the average of the notes is in tune, or it displays as only a few cents sharp or flat, don't mark anything.
   b. If the average of the notes is flat (more than 5 cents), write the number of cents flat; ie. -12
   c. If the average of the notes is sharp (more than 5 cents), write the number of cents sharp; ie. +12
3. Repeat step #2 for every note within the range of your instrument.
4. When you have completed the Check Sheet, go back to the notes that were MOST out of tune and learn solutions to play them in tune by improving tone, firming or relaxing your embouchure, using alternate fingerings, etc. If you have difficulty getting any particular notes in tune, please read the chapter *Factors Affecting Pitch*. When you revisit your Intonation Check-Sheet, ALWAYS USE YOUR **EARS** FIRST BEFORE YOUR EYES!

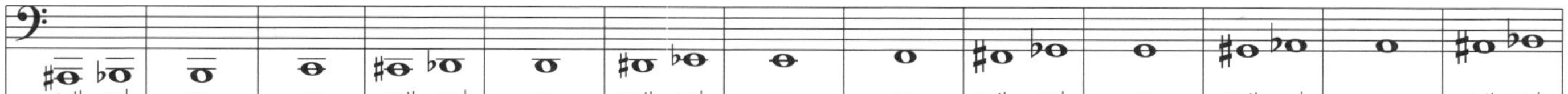

| | A# Bb | B | C | C# Db | D | D# Eb | E | F | F# Gb | G | G# Ab | A | A# Bb |
|---|---|---|---|---|---|---|---|---|---|---|---|---|---|
| **Number of cents flat (-) or sharp (+):** | - + | - + | - + | - + | - + | - + | - + | - + | - + | - + | - + | - + | - + |
| **Solutions:** | | | | | | | | | | | | | |

| | B | C | C# Db | D | D# Eb | E | F | F# Gb | G | G# Ab | A | A# Bb | B |
|---|---|---|---|---|---|---|---|---|---|---|---|---|---|
| **Number of cents flat (-) or sharp (+):** | - + | - + | - + | - + | - + | - + | - + | - + | - + | - + | - + | - + | - + |
| **Solutions:** | | | | | | | | | | | | | |

| | C | C# Db | D | D# Eb | E | F | F# Gb | G | G# Ab | A | A# Bb | B | C |
|---|---|---|---|---|---|---|---|---|---|---|---|---|---|
| **Number of cents flat (-) or sharp (+):** | - + | - + | - + | - + | - + | - + | - + | - + | - + | - + | - + | - + | - + |
| **Solutions:** | | | | | | | | | | | | | |

**Figure 7.6.** Horn Intonation Chart Template

## HORN INTONATION CHECK-SHEET

Name: _____

Mouthpiece: _____

Notes: _____

**Instructions:**

1. Properly warm up your instrument and then tune to A = 440.
2. Sustain a written note on your instrument 2 or 3 times in a row while a friend watches the tuner:
   a. If the average of the notes is in tune, or it displays as only a few cents sharp or flat, don't mark anything.
   b. If the average of the notes is flat (more than 5 cents), write the number of cents flat; ie. -12
   c. If the average of the notes is sharp (more than 5 cents), write the number of cents sharp; ie. +12
3. Repeat step #2 for every note within the range of your instrument.
4. When you have completed the Check Sheet, go back to the notes that were MOST out of tune and learn solutions to play them in tune by improving tone, firming or relaxing your embouchure, using alternate fingerings, etc. If you have difficulty getting any particular notes in tune, please read the chapter *Factors Affecting Pitch*. When you revisit your Intonation Check-Sheet, ALWAYS USE YOUR **EARS** FIRST BEFORE YOUR EYES!

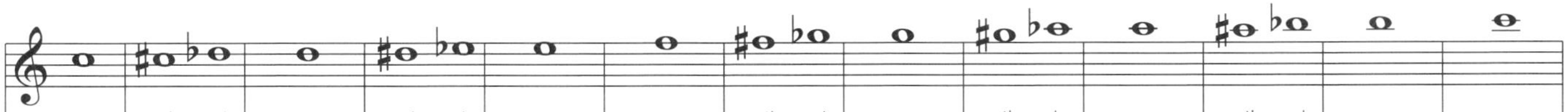

| | C | C♯ D♭ | D | D♯ E♭ | E | F | F♯ G♭ | G | G♯ A♭ | A | A♯ B♭ | B |
|---|---|---|---|---|---|---|---|---|---|---|---|---|
| **Number of cents flat (-) or sharp (+):** | - + | - + | - + | - + | - + | - + | - + | - + | - + | - + | - + | - + |
| **Solutions:** | | | | | | | | | | | | |

| | C | C♯ D♭ | D | D♯ E♭ | E | F | F♯ G♭ | G | G♯ A♭ | A | A♯ B♭ | B |
|---|---|---|---|---|---|---|---|---|---|---|---|---|
| **Number of cents flat (-) or sharp (+):** | - + | - + | - + | - + | - + | - + | - + | - + | - + | - + | - + | - + |
| **Solutions:** | | | | | | | | | | | | |

| | C | C♯ D♭ | D | D♯ E♭ | E | F | F♯ G♭ | G | G♯ A♭ | A | A♯ B♭ | C |
|---|---|---|---|---|---|---|---|---|---|---|---|---|
| **Number of cents flat (-) or sharp (+):** | - + | - + | - + | - + | - + | - + | - + | - + | - + | - + | - + | - + |
| **Solutions:** | | | | | | | | | | | | |

**Figure 7.7.** Trumpet Intonation Chart Template

# TRUMPET INTONATION CHECK-SHEET

Name: _____
Mouthpiece: _____
Notes: _____

**Instructions:**

1. Properly warm up your instrument and then tune to A = 440.
2. Sustain a written note on your instrument 2 or 3 times in a row while a friend watches the tuner:
   a. If the average of the notes is in tune, or it displays as only a few cents sharp or flat, don't mark anything.
   b. If the average of the notes is flat (more than 5 cents), write the number of cents flat; ie. -12
   c. If the average of the notes is sharp (more than 5 cents), write the number of cents sharp; ie. +12
3. Repeat step #2 for every note within the range of your instrument.
4. When you have completed the Check Sheet, go back to the notes that were MOST out of tune and learn solutions to play them in tune by improving tone, firming or relaxing your embouchure, using alternate fingerings, etc. If you have difficulty getting any particular notes in tune, please read the chapter *Factors Affecting Pitch*. When you revisit your Intonation Check-Sheet, ALWAYS USE YOUR **EARS** FIRST BEFORE YOUR EYES!

| | F# Gb | G | G# Ab | A | A# Bb | B | C | C# Db | D | D# Eb | E | F |
|---|---|---|---|---|---|---|---|---|---|---|---|---|
| **Number of cents flat (-) or sharp (+):** | - + | - + | - + | - + | - + | - + | - + | - + | - + | - + | - + | - + |
| **Solutions:** | | | | | | | | | | | | |

| | F# Gb | G | G# Ab | A | A# Bb | B | C | C# Db | D | D# Eb | E | F |
|---|---|---|---|---|---|---|---|---|---|---|---|---|
| **Number of cents flat (-) or sharp (+):** | - + | - + | - + | - + | - + | - + | - + | - + | - + | - + | - + | - + |
| **Solutions:** | | | | | | | | | | | | |

| | F# Gb | G | G# Ab | A | A# Bb | B | C | C# Db | D | D# Eb | E | F |
|---|---|---|---|---|---|---|---|---|---|---|---|---|
| **Number of cents flat (-) or sharp (+):** | - + | - + | - + | - + | - + | - + | - + | - + | - + | - + | - + | - + |
| **Solutions:** | | | | | | | | | | | | |

**Figure 7.8.** Trombone Intonation Chart Template

## TROMBONE INTONATION CHECK-SHEET

Name: _____

Mouthpiece: _____

Notes: _____

**Instructions:**

1. Properly warm up your instrument and then tune to A = 440.
2. Sustain a written note on your instrument 2 or 3 times in a row while a friend watches the tuner:
   a. If the average of the notes is in tune, or it displays as only a few cents sharp or flat, don't mark anything.
   b. If the average of the notes is flat (more than 5 cents), write the number of cents flat; ie. -12
   c. If the average of the notes is sharp (more than 5 cents), write the number of cents sharp; ie. +12
3. Repeat step #2 for every note within the range of your instrument.
4. When you have completed the Check Sheet, go back to the notes that were MOST out of tune and learn solutions to play them in tune by improving tone, firming or relaxing your embouchure, using alternate positions, etc. If you have difficulty getting any particular notes in tune, please read the chapter *Factors Affecting Pitch.* When you revisit your Intonation Check-Sheet, ALWAYS USE YOUR **EARS** FIRST BEFORE YOUR **EYES!**

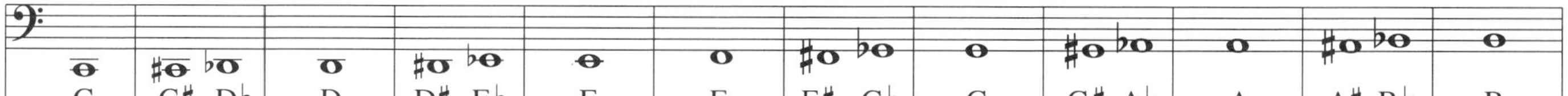

| | C | C♯ D♭ | D | D♯ E♭ | E | F | F♯ G♭ | G | G♯ A♭ | A | A♯ B♭ | B |
|---|---|---|---|---|---|---|---|---|---|---|---|---|
| **Number of cents flat (-) or sharp (+):** | - + | - + | - + | - + | - + | - + | - + | - + | - + | - + | - + | - + |
| **Solutions:** | | | | | | | | | | | | |

| | C | C♯ D♭ | D | D♯ E♭ | E | F | F♯ G♭ | G | G♯ A♭ | A | A♯ B♭ | B |
|---|---|---|---|---|---|---|---|---|---|---|---|---|
| **Number of cents flat (-) or sharp (+):** | - + | - + | - + | - + | - + | - + | - + | - + | - + | - + | - + | - + |
| **Solutions:** | | | | | | | | | | | | |

| | C | C♯ D♭ | D | D♯ E♭ | E | F | F♯ G♭ | G | G♯ A♭ | A | A♯ B♭ | C |
|---|---|---|---|---|---|---|---|---|---|---|---|---|
| **Number of cents flat (-) or sharp (+):** | - + | - + | - + | - + | - + | - + | - + | - + | - + | - + | - + | - + |
| **Solutions:** | | | | | | | | | | | | |

**Figure 7.9.** Euphonium Intonation Chart Template

## EUPHONIUM INTONATION CHECK-SHEET

Name: _____
Mouthpiece: _____
Notes:

**Instructions:**

1. Properly warm up your instrument and then tune to A = 440.
2. Sustain a written note on your instrument 2 or 3 times in a row while a friend watches the tuner:
   a. If the average of the notes is in tune, or it displays as only a few cents sharp or flat, don't mark anything.
   b. If the average of the notes is flat (more than 5 cents), write the number of cents flat; ie. -12
   c. If the average of the notes is sharp (more than 5 cents), write the number of cents sharp; ie. +12
3. Repeat step #2 for every note within the range of your instrument.
4. When you have completed the Check Sheet, go back to the notes that were MOST out of tune and learn solutions to play them in tune by improving tone, firming or relaxing your embouchure, using alternate fingerings, etc.
   If you have difficulty getting any particular notes in tune, please read the chapter *Factors Affecting Pitch*.
   When you revisit your Intonation Check-Sheet, ALWAYS USE YOUR **EARS** FIRST BEFORE YOUR EYES!

| | A# Bb | B | C | C# Db | D | D# Eb | E | F | F# Gb | G | G# Ab | A | A# Bb |
|---|---|---|---|---|---|---|---|---|---|---|---|---|---|
| Number of cents flat (-) or sharp (+): | - + | - + | - + | - + | - + | - + | - + | - + | - + | - + | - + | - + | - + |
| Solutions: | | | | | | | | | | | | | |

| | B | C | C# Db | D | D# Eb | E | F | F# Gb | G | G# Ab | A | A# Bb | B |
|---|---|---|---|---|---|---|---|---|---|---|---|---|---|
| Number of cents flat (-) or sharp (+): | - + | - + | - + | - + | - + | - + | - + | - + | - + | - + | - + | - + | - + |
| Solutions: | | | | | | | | | | | | | |

| | C | C# Db | D | D# Eb | E | F | F# Gb | G | G# Ab | A | A# Bb | B | C |
|---|---|---|---|---|---|---|---|---|---|---|---|---|---|
| Number of cents flat (-) or sharp (+): | - + | - + | - + | - + | - + | - + | - + | - + | - + | - + | - + | - + | - + |
| Solutions: | | | | | | | | | | | | | |

**Figure 7.10.** Tuba Intonation Chart Template

# TUBA INTONATION CHECK-SHEET

Name: _____
Mouthpiece: _____
Notes: _____

**Instructions:**
1. Properly warm up your instrument and then tune to A = 440.
2. Sustain a written note on your instrument 2 or 3 times in a row while a friend watches the tuner:
   a. If the average of the notes is in tune, or it displays as only a few cents sharp or flat, don't mark anything.
   b. If the average of the notes is flat (more than 5 cents), write the number of cents flat; ie. -12
   c. If the average of the notes is sharp (more than 5 cents), write the number of cents sharp; ie. +12
3. Repeat step #2 for every note within the range of your instrument.
4. When you have completed the Check Sheet, go back to the notes that were MOST out of tune and learn solutions to play them in tune by improving tone, firming or relaxing your embouchure, using alternate fingerings, etc. If you have difficulty getting any particular notes in tune, please read the chapter *Factors Affecting Pitch*. When you revisit your Intonation Check-Sheet, ALWAYS USE YOUR **EARS** FIRST BEFORE YOUR **EYES!**

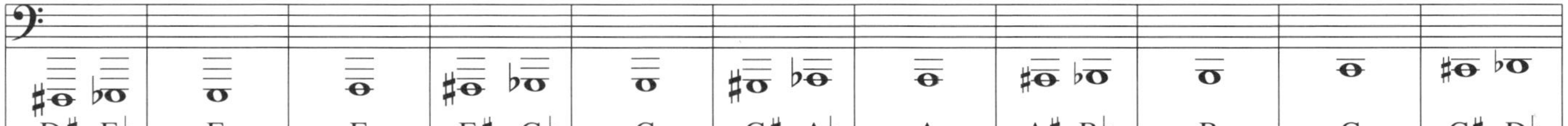

| | D♯ E♭ | E | F | F♯ G♭ | G | G♯ A♭ | A | A♯ B♭ | B | C | C♯ D♭ |
|---|---|---|---|---|---|---|---|---|---|---|---|
| **Number of cents flat (-) or sharp (+):** | - + | - + | - + | - + | - + | - + | + | - + | - + | - + | - + |
| **Solutions:** | | | | | | | | | | | |

| | D  D♯ E♭ | E | F  F♯ G♭ | G  G♯ A♭ | A  A♯ B♭ | B | C  C♯ D♭ |
|---|---|---|---|---|---|---|---|
| **Number of cents flat (-) or sharp (+):** | - + - + | - + | - + - + | - + - + | - + - + | - + | - + - + |
| **Solutions:** | | | | | | | |

| | D  D♯ E♭ | E | F  F♯ G♭ | G  G♯ A♭ | A  A♯ B♭ | B | C  C♯ D♭ |
|---|---|---|---|---|---|---|---|
| **Number of cents flat (-) or sharp (+):** | + - + | + | + - + | - + - + | + - + | - + | - + - + |
| **Solutions:** | | | | | | | |

# PART 8

# Tuning—An Ongoing Process

Tuning is not just something we do at the beginning of each rehearsal. Tuning is an ongoing process. In other words, tuning at the beginning of rehearsal is used to place the instruments at their correct length, and to *wake up* the ears for active listening. The remainder of the rehearsal includes an ongoing attention to fitting each pitch within the sounding overtones of the ensemble by listening down to the lowest voices. In order to achieve such beat-less tuning, students must learn how to manually adjust their pitch by such means as air, embouchure, alternate fingerings, rolling of headjoint (flutes), etc. However, along with learning how to make pitch adjustments, players must also understand the various factors that affect pitch (Table 8.1).

## I SAID LISTEN! . . . BUT WHAT EXACTLY ARE WE TO LISTEN FOR?

When asking students to *listen* they must know what it is they are *listening* for? They must listen for the lowest voice and be able to *balance* all the upper voices relative to this lowest pitch or fundamental pitch. Students should listen to the lower voices to balance their pitch, as it is easier to match pitch with lower voices than it is with higher voices. After teaching this concept of *listening down* for the pitch, students will know that those playing first parts should listen down to those playing second and third parts. Each player must perform louder than those playing higher notes, and perform softer than those playing lower notes.

Based on the above concept, one may consider that much responsibility is placed on the tuba players to provide the in-tune fundamental for the remainder of the players to balance their pitch within. YES, there is great responsibility on the tuba players. (This is why I prefer to tune the ensemble by using the tubas to sound the tuning pitch.) If the tubas are incorrect then the entire ensemble will be incorrect. (In the same aspect, the timpani player must also be just as accurate in tuning, as are the tuba players.) In order for any instrument to play as close to correct pitch as possible, each instrument must be at its correct length where it is acoustically constructed to play best in tune. When tuning the instrument to a strobe, any physical adjustments of air speed, embouchure, alternate fingerings, etc. should be avoided. Only use these adjustments while actually performing music, not while tuning the instrument to its best note and instrument length.

## FACTORS AFFECTING PITCH

**Table 8.1.** Factors Affecting Pitch

☹ = unsatisfactory result and cause
☺ = solution to achieve a satisfactory result

| | |
|---|---|
| **Air** | ☹ *slow, weak air speed = unsupported tone which can cause pitch to go flat; OR if the slow air causes player to play too soft, then the pitch can go sharp for reed instruments*<br>☹ *fast, exaggerated air speed = can cause pitch to go sharp for brass instruments and flute OR if the fast air causes player to play too loud, then the pitch can go flat for reed instruments.*<br>☺ steady, focused air speed = centered and supported pitch |
| **Posture** | ☹ *poor posture = poor tone and thus poor pitch*<br>☺ correct posture = centered and supported pitch |
| **Embouchure** | ☹ *weak and poorly developed embouchure = saggy, flabby tone which can cause pitch to go flat*<br>☹ *tight, biting or forced embouchure = thin, restricted tone which can cause pitch to go sharp*<br>☹ *flute: air stream directed too far down = flat pitch; air stream directed too far up = sharp pitch*<br>☺ correctly formed embouchure and direction of air stream = centered and supported pitch |
| **Mouthpiece** | Selection of a quality mouthpiece **affects intonation more than any other factor**. Even the same brand/model of mouthpiece can have varying results in tone and pitch. Work closely with a trusted artist teacher to find the best mouthpiece for every instrument. Most beginning instruments are supplied with a stock mouthpiece, which typically produce less than satisfactory results; encourage students/parents to purchase a step-up mouthpiece. |
| **Amount of Mouthpiece** | ☹ *too much mouthpiece in mouth = wide, uncontrolled tone plays flat*<br>☹ *too little mouthpiece in mouth = small, restricted tone induces biting which causes pitch to play sharp*<br>☹ *flute: too much lower lip on plate = flat pitch; too little lower lip on plate = sharp pitch*<br>☹ *oboe/bassoon: too much reed in mouth = shortened instrument that causes pitch to play sharp; too little reed in mouth = lengthened instrument that causes pitch to play flat*<br>☺ correct amount of mouthpiece taken in or covered = full and centered pitch<br>☺ oboe: if playing flat, cut off tip of reed, or take a little more reed into mouth; if playing sharp, pull tube out slightly (but never more than 1/8th of an inch, or take a little less reed into mouth<br>☺ bassoon: same as oboe except you should NOT adjust length of reed |
| **Angle of Mouthpiece** | ☹ *angle too far forward = poorly supported embouchure control on reed which causes pitch to go flat*<br>☹ *angle too far back = poor embouchure and too much pressure on reed which causes pitch to go sharp*<br>☺ correct angle of mouthpiece = full and centered pitch |
| **Lay of Mouthpiece** | ☹ *mouthpiece with a close lay = restriction of embouchure adjustment which causes pitch to play sharp*<br>☹ *mouthpiece with an open lay = too much room for embouchure adjustment which causes pitch to play flat*<br>☺ mouthpiece with a medium lay and medium tip opening = ability for embouchure to more easily control pitch |
| **Barrel and Bocal Length** | ☹ *barrel/bocal too long = lengthened instrument that will play flat*<br>☹ *barrel/bocal too short = shortened instrument that will play sharp*<br>☺ proper barrel/bocal length = ability for embouchure to more easily control pitch; recommended clarinet barrel length is 66 mm; recommended standard bassoon bocal length is a #2 (#3 on Fox models) (the higher the number the longer the bocal) |
| **Horn Hand Position** | ☹ *right hand held too far in = closing of bell causes pitch to play flat*<br>☹ *right hand held too far out = opening of bell causes pitch to play sharp*<br>☹ *fully stopped horn = causes pitch to play 1/2-step higher*<br>☺ correct hand position = centered pitch |
| **Tongue Position** | High arch in tongue will cause pitch to play higher.<br>Low arch in tongue will cause pitch to play lower. |
| **Reed Condition** | ☹ *reed too soft = weak reed that plays below pitch, and encourages over-blowing which causes pitch to go flat*<br>☹ *reed too hard = encourages biting, therefore it causes pitch to go sharp*<br>☺ properly conditioned reed = able to control pitch |

*continues*

| | |
|---|---|
| **Equipment** | ☹ *poor equipment = poor pitch; often caused by inferior-made instruments; leaking tone holes; bent rods; poor mechanism alignment; poor quality mouthpiece or percussion mallet; poor reed; poorly adjusted percussion heads, stuck slides, etc.*<br>☹ *a pad that is too closed will cause pitch to play flat, while a pad too open will cause pitch to play sharp*<br>☺ good equipment = good pitch; caused by purchasing quality director-recommended instruments and equipment, proper care and maintenance by the student, and by annual maintenance by a qualified instrument technician. |
| **Dynamics** | ☹ *louder dynamics = encourages pitch to play sharp\**<br>☹ *softer dynamics = encourages pitch to play flat\**<br>\* *opposite pitch tendency for reed instruments, esp. saxophone and clarinet. (Although this pitch tendency can sometimes vary dependent on reed strength and embouchure.)*<br>☺ when playing at louder dynamics, compensate for flat pitch by firming the embouchure; (flutes will compensate for a sharp pitch by directing air stream down and/or rolling head-joint in)<br>☺ when playing at softer dynamics, compensate for sharp pitch by relaxing the embouchure; (flutes will compensate for a flat pitch by directing air stream up and/or rolling head-joint out) |
| **Pitch Concept** | ☹ *poor pitch concept = poor pitch; caused by lack of interval understanding and poor knowledge of the concept of beat-less tuning*<br>☺ good pitch concept = good pitch; caused by frequent and regular singing and playing of intervals, practice of beat-less tuning, learning the *scale* of their instrument; and developing the ability to adjust pitch by means of embouchure and alternate fingerings |
| **Balance** | ☹ *poor balance = poor sound + poor intonation; caused by players trying to hear themselves above others instead of with others; poor balance can often be an ensemble mix of under-supported and over-blown sounds that create distorted pitch*<br>☺ proper balance = good tone + good pitch; caused by quality tone production achieving the fundamental concepts of blend and balance, and allowing a mature sound that can be clearly heard by players that may need to adjust pitch tendencies to the specific chord in question |
| **Timpani Pitch** | ☹ *unequal head tension = poor pitch*<br>☺ equal head tension = timpani in tune with itself<br>☹ *difficulty tuning timpani = poor pitch*<br>☺ ease of tuning = good pitch; caused by frequent and regular singing and playing of intervals |
| **Percussion** | Pitch can be affected by quality of drumheads and quality of mallet instrument bars. Choose appropriate sticks and mallets, and learn to accurately tune batter heads. |
| **Temperature** | ☹ *colder temperatures = flat pitch in wind instruments, but sharp pitch in string instruments*<br>☹ *warmer temperatures = sharp pitch in wind instruments, but flat pitch in string instruments*<br>☺ whenever possible, warm-up the ensemble in the actual performance hall; instruct students that larger instruments and those instruments made of more metal than wood will change temperatures more drastically and thus their pitch will be the most affected; instruments are tested and tuned at 72 degrees Fahrenheit / 22 degrees Celsius in the factories |

## CLARINET TUNING AND THROAT TONES

Part of the difficulty of tuning the clarinet is the fact that it is the only cylindrical woodwind instrument that vibrates in odd partials only (especially in the lower register); in other words, it acts as a closed tube. In simplest terms, the conical bore of oboes, bassoons and saxophones create a node near the end of the tube that results in a full set of harmonic modes. However, the cylindrical tube of the clarinet acts as a quarter-wavelength resonator, which results in one-half tubing like the flute (Gibson, 1998). The clarinet overblows a twelfth by skipping even-numbered partials. This creates greater intonation problems for the clarinet than the saxophone or oboe, which has an octave key (8va) versus a register key (12th).

There are two reasons why clarinets are manufactured so that throat tones play higher than the remaining tones:

1.  Throat tones are more sensitive to changes in barrel length.

2.  Throat tones are usually played with resonance fingerings which helps lower the pitch (Ridenour, 2000).

Throat tone G is one of the best tuning notes on the clarinet as this open note puts the instrument best in tune with itself. This note should be tuned *first* by adjusting the length of the barrel. Then a closed note such as clarion C should be tuned *second* by adjusting the length of the middle joint. Players should never use the mouthpiece to adjust intonation on the clarinet.

The throat tones on the clarinet (G through Bb) bridge the gap between the missing octave and fifth. Throat tones on clarinet are *highly* variable. With beginners, the clarinet tends to play sharp in the throat tones; these pitch tendencies are generally the result of a stock mouthpiece. However, if a student plays on a quality mouthpiece and/or low pitch mouthpiece, they can actually play flat on throat tones. (The fingering chart in this book provides suggested fingerings for throat tones if they are sharp *or* flat.)

Russell A. Pizer in *How to Improve the High School Band Sound* says

> It has been said that if one were to improve the intonation of just the clarinet section the general intonation of the band would be improved by at least one-third. It is the clarinet section that is the largest. It is this section that not only carries the most melodic materials and lines but also does a great deal of accompanying of melodic lines being played by other sections and instruments. The clarinet section of the band can be compared in importance with the violin section of the orchestra (Pizer, 1976, p. 133).

## BRASS PITCH AND THE HARMONIC SERIES

An instrument's sound is constructed of the naturally occurring intervals present in the harmonic series, and the intonation tendencies of an instrument are influenced by these intervals. The composition of the harmonic series (Figure 8.1) follows the same set of intervals for every fundamental pitch:

P8 – P5 – P4 – M3 – m3 – m3 – M2 – M2 – M2 – M2 – m2 – M2 – m2 – m2 – m2 — (partials continue to get smaller and closer together).

**Figure 8.1.** Harmonic Series Pitch Tendencies

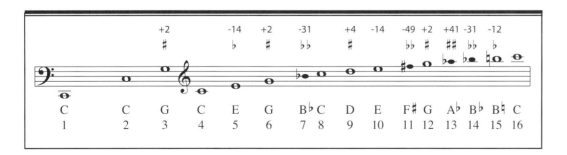

The addition of valves to brass instruments allowed players additional fundamentals, which offered an enhanced range of notes to sound. Valves create seven possible combinations (0 – 2 – 1 – 12 – 23 – 13 – 123) that make a brass instrument fully chromatic by the utilization of seven harmonic series.

Although the valve system greatly improved the melodic and technical efficiency of brass instruments, it also created pitch problems in that the combination of valves causes sharpness. In other words, as the vibrating air column (tubing) becomes longer then the degree of sharpness increases. The pitch tendencies for notes in the harmonic series based on the Third Partial are slightly sharp, the Fifth Partial is flat, the Sixth Partial is slightly sharp, and the Seventh Partial is extremely flat. In order to help correct this problem, most trumpets are fitted with both a first and third valve trigger/ring, and many euphoniums are equipped with a compensating fourth valve.

## SINGING AS A MEANS TO IMPROVING INTONATION

Singing with your band and orchestra is an effective method to improving both tone quality and intonation. Young musicians invariably play with a better tone and sense of pitch immediately after singing a passage. It is discouraging to visit a school where the players all giggle with embarrassment if they are asked to sing anything during the instrumental clinic. It is too apparent that these students do not sing as a regular part of their rehearsal and they are not comfortable with being asked to do so. All too often, such ensembles play consistently out of tune and with a poor to mediocre tone quality. On the other hand, ensembles that are comfortable with singing as part of a regular rehearsal routine often have a more mature tone quality and increased skills to improve intonation flaws.

Warm-up routines can be created to include singing as a regular activity. Singing intervals and scales develop an increased awareness of pitch and interval relationships. In addition, there are advantages to singing motifs and melodies in current repertoire that the ensemble is preparing. Ed Lisk's book *Alternative Rehearsal Techniques* provides many exercises that adhere well to both singing and playing. Singing also has merit for rehearsing rhythmic precision.

Richard Franko Goldman (1961) in *The Wind Band* says *the fact that the player can match his Bb to another one simply is no guarantee that he can play C or D in tune, because in most cases he has never learned intervals* (p. 249). The student must understand and know how to sing and play simple intervals and chords before he can play in tune. The best way to be able to play intervals in tune is to be able to sing intervals in tune. The more practice we have at singing intervals the better able we will be in the audiation process before actually sounding the note.

Students should first practice playing unisons in tune (with a drone on a tuner or keyboard), followed by the practice of open octave intervals, then perfect fifths, major thirds and minor thirds. The concept of balance comes into play when recognizing and tuning intervals. In other words, students must remember to fit the higher sounding notes into the lower sounding notes. Once the correct balance is achieved, it is much easier to recognize the interval and make appropriate adjustments.

If your school provides a music theory course, then it is imperative that you provide sight-singing activities. Such theory courses should include solfege as the traditional aural training and sight-singing method. Solfeggio is the practice of singing using solfa syllables (do-re-mi-fa-sol-la-ti-do). By learning the art of Solfege, a student learns to recognize harmonic and melodic intervals. The system provides a theoretical and musical method to identify relationships between notes and chords. Aural recognition is a necessary skill for the accomplished ensemble, and players must learn to accurately hear intervals, chords, and harmonic progressions. Stephen Melillo's *Function Chorales* (http://www.storm-world.com) are a great tool for your ensemble to explore and develop interval recognition and harmonic progression. *Treasury of Scales* (Belwin) is another great ensemble resource as exercises include all major and minor scales harmonized in SATB format.

## "ALL I REALLY NEED TO KNOW I LEARNED IN" CHAMBER MUSIC

You may remember a bestseller book a number of years ago titled *All I Really Need to Know I Learned in Kindergarten*. Similarly, the author believes that all we really need to know in music can be acquired through participation in chamber music. Having grown up in a less than mediocre band program, the author arrived at college with little or no experience in the concepts of tone, balance, blend, intonation, style, and quality music making. She remembers quite vividly her first experience sitting in a full wind ensemble with balanced instrumentation. (Ah! So that is what a horn sounds like? Ah! So that is what a chord sounds like when all the parts are present?) As much as the author learned from performing with the college wind ensemble, she learned a great deal more about being a musician as a member of the university saxophone quartet. There was nowhere to hide poor tone or pitch in a chamber group. Yikes! There was no room for error when it came to producing improper style or articulation. And certainly you had to be fully cognizant of pulse, rhythm, and tempo. The four players learned a great deal from the opportunity to coach themselves. In a large ensemble, it is easy to be spoon-fed musical instruction from the conductor, but in a chamber group, players are responsible for their own musical instruction. Ears become vibrantly alive and aware of parts beyond the page in order to arrive at a truly artistic chamber music product.

Participation in chamber ensembles is one of the best ways to develop an individual's tone and intonation skill. It is all too simple for a student to hide faulty tone and pitch in a large ensemble, yet such weaknesses are exposed when playing in small ensembles. Players have no choice but to improve their pitch and tone, unless they are satisfied with "sticking out" in the group. Teachers must encourage students to participate in duets, trios, quartets and other small ensemble settings. Provide an opportunity for public performance of student ensembles at school, church, and community events. Be creative! Organize a Chamber Music Club!

## DRONES

Using the tool of a sustained pitch (drone) is one of the best methods for training the ear and developing the flexibility for *placing* a note in tune. A drone will remain constant in frequency whereas a human drone (voice or wind instrument), no matter how professional the player, will always have subtle changes in frequency. The use an electronic drone is constant and a player will be able to hear *beats* between the two sounding pitches. A suggested routine for practicing with drones (Figure 8.2) is as follows:

1.  Begin with unisons with the goal of eliminating all *beats* in your sound with the drone.

    ■  Start with unisons that are *reliable* notes on your instrument. Once you are able to match these unisons, move to matching all notes within the range of your instrument.

2.  Move to matching perfect fifths and fourths, again with the goal of eliminating all *beats* in your sound with the drone. In order to do so, you will need to adjust your sound approximately two cents higher from ET for fifths, and two cents lower for fourths.

3.  Match major thirds by eliminating all sounding beats. In order to do so, you will need to adjust your sound approximately fourteen cents lower from ET.

4.  Match minor thirds by eliminating all sounding beats by adjusting your sound approximately sixteen cents higher from ET.

---

**Figure 8.2.** Drone Exercise—Intervals

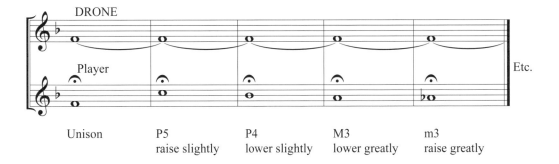

5.  Continue with other intervals.

6.  Practice arpeggios (Figure 8.3) against the drone.

---

**Figure 8.3.** Drone Exercise—Arpeggio

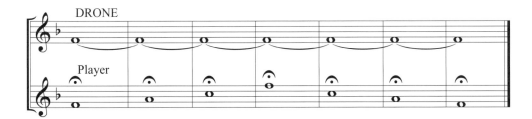

7.   Practice scales (Figure 8.4) using the drone as a pedal point.

**Figure 8.4.** Drone Exercise—Scale

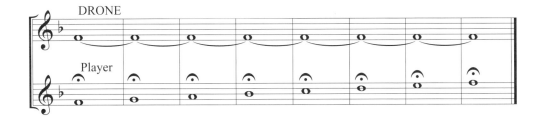

The more you work with drones, the more your ear will become refined along with the ability to immediately *place* a note in tune, versus simply playing a note and then slowly navigating your way through a number of adjustments to play the note in tune.

There are several resources available for practicing with drones:

- electronic keyboards

- electronic chromatic tuners

- recorded CDs

- music notation software

- free and paid downloadable audio files from websites

- free and paid applications for smart phones and tablets

## MOUTHPIECE/REED/EMBOUCHURE PITCH

Like snowflakes, no two mouthpieces, reeds or headjoints are *exactly* identical. Even the same brand and model will have minute differences that a trained ear and musician will hear and feel. The mouthpiece/reed/headjoint is arguably the most important piece of equipment on the instrument. For example, you can put a poor quality mouthpiece on an excellent quality instrument and still only sound from poor to mediocre in pitch and tone. When purchasing a new instrument or upgrading your mouthpiece/reed/headjoint, it is best to ask a local expert for assistance in selecting the best equipment. Tone quality and pitch can be affected not only by various facings, lays, tip openings, bores, cuts (hand vs. factory), tone-holes, lengths, etc. but also by the material used in construction. Flute headjoints can be metal, silver, gold, platinum, etc.; clarinet and saxophone mouthpieces can be plastic, rubber, crystal, glass, etc.

A correctly developed embouchure is imperative for the progress of quality tone and centered pitch. Of course many factors come into play to achieve the goal of *placing* the correct sound quality and pitch. Such factors include a good quality instrument, proper mouthpiece, appropriate use of air, shape of oral cavity, and tongue position. One consideration to check a player's correct embouchure development is to monitor an average pitch they should get on their reed alone or mouthpiece and reed alone (Table 8.2). Use this chart to check your student's pitch from time to time. Although the mouthpiece pitch references are not standard practice by every instructor, they do serve as a useful pedagogical tool.

**Table 8.2.** Recommended Pitch Production Practice on Mouthpiece/Reed/Headjoint Alone

| Instrument | Concert Pitch on Mouthpiece / Reed / Headjoint Alone |
|---|---|
| Flute | A: on stopped or open headjoint; this is a good average pitch for young flutists to practice sustaining a controlled open sound. More advanced students could practice playing octaves in tune and then learn to raise and lower each pitch by as many cents as possible. |
| Oboe | C:  Reed alone should "crow" octave C's |
| Clarinet | C:  on Soprano<br>F♯: on Bass    *Note: Pitch should be within +/- half step of pitch indicated.* |
| Saxophone | C:  on Soprano<br>A:  on Alto    *Note: Pitch should be within +/- half step of pitch indicated.*<br>G:  on Tenor<br>D:  on Baritone |
| Bassoon | G or A:  Reed alone should "crow" a G or A |

**Note:** Information compiled from interviews with selected professional music educators/artists.

Practicing pitch flexibility on the mouthpiece alone is of course an excellent exercise for brass players, but is equally effective for saxophonists and clarinets. (Please remember that when the clarinet is assembled it has very little pitch flexibility due to its nature of only overblowing odd partials.) When practicing pitch flexibility on the mouthpiece alone some points to consider include:

- Use a fast, consistent air speed.

- Try to generate the pitch bending with a combination of air, oral cavity, and tongue position. Movement in the jaw should be kept as minimal as possible.

- Everyone has a different shaped throat and tongue so it is important to experiment with various positions to see how it affects your sound and pitch. Move slowly through the vowels *a – e – i – o – u* and listen carefully to the changes you hear.

- Alternate between singing the pitches and then playing the pitches on your mouthpiece.

## LONG TONES, OVERTONES, HARMONICS AND LIP SLURS

Another excellent method for developing correct *placement* of notes is to request students practice performing long tones, overtones, harmonics and lip slurs. The use of long tones and proper breathing is an indispensible tool for every wind instrument. Barry M. Shank shares his view on musical breathing:

> The exhaling process is the most important breathing facet in playing, since it is blowing which produces the sound. . . . A good singer does not imagine 'pushing' with his diaphragm or, as he sings, tightening his abdominal muscles. What does he do? A trained singer takes advantage of his frontal resonating chambers in order to produce a big, resonant, articulate sound. Wind players are no different. They also must make use of the facial bone structure. (Shank, 1963, p. 30)

The value of practicing long tones cannot be overestimated. Students should spend at least five minutes each day producing long tones in varying registers and at varying dynamics with the purest of tone possible. Achieving the characteristic sound expected for each instrument is directly related to the student's ability to perform a clear *fundamental pitch* enhanced by all the resonating *overtones*. Of course there will be musical situations that call for a flexibility of tonal color, but a player must be first accomplished in the ability to perform a *pure* tone before truly encompassing a *flexible* tone.

Daily practice must be invested in ridding the tone of any obtrusive factors that may generate a tight or sloppy or fuzzy sound. Any unpleasant tone must be analyzed for possible interfering factors. Do not allow your *personal ears* to be trained to accept distasteful tones or a sound that is less than its pure potential. Students may defend that they know the tone isn't that great but they just do not have the time to fix their reed, or embouchure, or whatever factor may be contributing to the resultant tone. The "I'll fix it later" attitude only contributes to training the personal ears to not be offended by poor tone quality. Take the extra time now to refine tone in order to contribute to all aspects of improving pitch.

Always practice long tone exercises (Figure 8.5) with the use of a tuner in order to learn pitch tendencies in all registers and at all dynamic levels.

**Figure 8.5.** Example of Long Tone Exercise

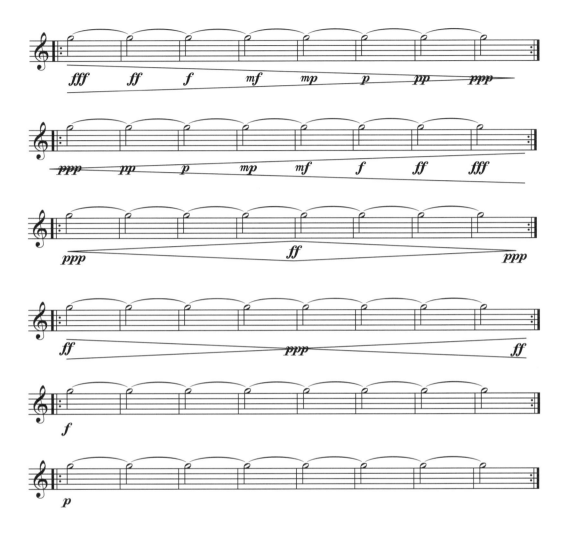

Natural harmonics or overtones may be practiced on a specific instrument as follows:

**Brass**

Figure 8.6 is just one of many examples of a lip slur exercise. When playing the exercise, use air speed, voicing (throat/oral cavity), tongue position to generate each overtone. You must allow for lip flexibility, but try to move your embouchure as little as possible.

**Figure 8.6.** Example of Brass Lip Slur Exercise

## Flute

Figure 8.7 is just one of many examples of a harmonic exercise. When playing the exercise use a consistent air stream, allow the bottom and top lip to move forward, and keep the corners of embouchure flexible. Air speed will need to slightly increase as you move to the higher harmonics. Playing harmonics on the flute assist in developing proper embouchure, air support, pitch and tone quality.

**Figure 8.7.** Example of Flute Harmonic Exercise

Finger low C - - - - - - - - - - - - - - - - - - - - - - - - - - - - - - - - - - - - - -

Many excellent resources are available for finding more information on practicing harmonics; (not an inclusive list):

Dick, Robert. (1989). *The Other Flute—A Performance Manual of Contemporary Technique.* St. Louis, MO: MMB Music.

Dick, Robert. (2008). *Tone Development Through Extended Technique.* St. Louis, MO: MMB Music; Multiple Breath Music Company.

Levine, Carin and Christina Mitropoulos-Bott. (2009). *The Techniques of Flute Playing*, (3rd edition).

Moyse, Marcel. (1934). *De La Sonorite.* Paris: Leduc Publishing.

Robison, Paula. (1989). *The Paula Robison Flute Warmups Book.* European American Music Corporation.

Wye, Trevor. (2003 CD edition). *Practice Book for the Flute, Volume 1: Tone.* New York, NY: Schirmer.

Wye, Trevor. (2003 CD edition). *Practice Book for the Flute Volume 4: Intonation and Vibrato.* New York, NY: Schirmer.

## Clarinet

Figure 8.8 is just one of many examples of an overtone exercise. When playing the exercise, use air speed, voicing (throat/oral cavity), and tongue position to generate each overtone. Keep your embouchure as still as possible.

**Figure 8.8.** Example of Clarinet Overtone Exercise

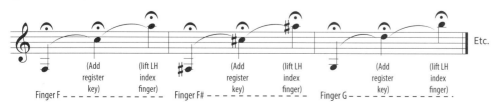

(The above patterns can also be *voiced* while only fingering the lower note.)

Many excellent resources are available for finding more information on practicing overtones; (not an inclusive list):

Drushler, Paul (1978). *The Altissimo Register: A partial approach: for soprano clarinet.* Shall-u-mo Publications.

Gingras, Michele (2006). *Clarinet Secrets—52 Performance Strategies for the Advanced Clarinetist.* Scarecrow Press, Inc.: Lanham, MD.

Gingras, Michele (2011). *More Clarinet Secrets: 100 Quick Tips for the Advanced Clarinetist.* Scarecrow Press, Inc.: Lanham, MD.

Guy, Larry (1996). *Intonation Training for Clarinetists.* (3rd ed.) Stony Point, NY: Rivernote Press.

Heim, Norman M. (1976). *The Development of the Altissimo Register for Clarinet.* Delevan, NY: Kendor Music.

Ridenour, Thomas (1986). *The Annotated Book of Altissimo Clarinet Fingerings.* Duncanville, TX: Tom's Clarinet Service.

Ridenour, Thomas (2002). *The Educator's Guide to the Clarinet.* Duncanville, TX: Tom's Clarinet Service.

**Saxophone**

Figure 8.9 is just one of many examples of an overtone exercise. When playing the exercise, use air speed, voicing (throat/oral cavity), and tongue position to generate each overtone. Although there will be increased firmness on the embouchure when playing higher harmonics, keep your embouchure as still as possible.

**Figure 8.9.** Example of Saxophone Overtone Exercise

Many excellent resources are available for finding more information on practicing overtones; (not an inclusive list):

Cohen, Paul. (2007). *The Altissimo Primer.* Teaneck, NJ: To the Fore Publishers.

Lang, Rosemary. (1971; out of print). *Saxophone: Beginning Studies in the Altissimo Register.* Indianapolis, IN: Lang Music Publications.

Liebman, David. (1994). *Developing a Personal Saxophone Sound,* (2nd edition). Medfield, MA: Dorn Publications.

Luckey, Robert A. (1998). *Saxophone Altissimo: High Note Development for the Contemporary Player,* (2nd edition). Lafayette, LA: Olympia Music.

Rascher, Sigurd M. (1994). *Top-Tones for the Saxophone: Four-Octave Range,* (3rd edition). New York, NY: Carl Fischer Music. [This book is more specific to older Buescher horns.]

Rousseau, Eugene (2002). *Saxophone High Tones: A Systematic Approach to the Extension of the Range of All the Saxophones,* (2nd edition). St. Louis, MO: MMB Music.

Sinta, Donald J. and Denise C. Dabney. (1992). *Voicing: An Approach to the Saxophone's Third Register.* Laurel, MD: Sintafest Music Company.

## THE PITCH BAROMETER: MONITORING INTONATION SKILLS

The following *recipe* is reprinted with permission from *The Music Director's Cookbook: Creative Recipes for a Successful Program* (2005) and published by Meredith Music Publications.

# The Pitch Barometer—Measuring Intonation Skills

Monitoring the pitch accuracy of players in a large ensemble is especially difficult when we are often limited in our rehearsal time. How then do we measure the pitch-matching skills of each and every player in our group? Does this sound like a formidable task? It doesn't have to be. Try this recipe to evaluate your student's intonation skills.

### INGREDIENTS:
Ensure that instruments are properly warmed up before making this recipe. Players should be able to play a few basic scales and identify and perform various intervals in the scale key.

### SERVES:
All instrumental and voice students.

### INSTRUCTIONS:
It is impossible, and quite frankly a waste of time, to go around the room with a tuner to every player. Even if you had the time during a rehearsal to do this, you really have only assured yourself of one thing—you can be somewhat comfortable knowing that every player is at least *close* to sounding in tune on a unison concert B-flat, or whichever concert note you decide to tune. However, there is never any guarantee that the players will all sound this close to tune on any other note they play during rehearsal. We all understand that each brand/make and type of wind instrument comes packaged with its own intonation tendencies. Just as no two snowflakes are ever identical, so too are no two saxophones or two horns, etc. ever truly identical in how they sound pitch.

Singing with your band and orchestra is an effective method to improving both tone quality and intonation. Young musicians invariably play with a better tone and sense of pitch immediately after singing a passage. Warm-up routines can be created to include singing as a regular activity. Singing intervals and scales develops an increased awareness of pitch and interval relationships. The best way to be able to play intervals in tune is to be able to sing intervals in tune. In addition, there are advantages to singing motifs and melodies in current repertoire that the ensemble is preparing. Singing also has merit for rehearsing rhythmic precision. The more practice we have at singing intervals, the better able we will be in the *audiation* process before actually sounding the note.

Students should first practice playing unisons in tune, followed by open octave intervals, then perfect fifths, major thirds, and minor thirds. The concept of balance comes into play when recognizing and tuning intervals. In other words, students must remember to fit the higher sounding notes into the lower sounding notes. Once the correct balance is achieved, it is much easier to recognize the interval and make appropriate adjustments.

Now it is time to use your *Pitch Barometer*. Here is how it works. Periodically monitor pitches of individual players by instructing the entire ensemble to sustain a unison pitch and then point to one player to continue sustaining the pitch while the other players release their sound. (Strive to create a friendly learning atmosphere while using the *Pitch Barometer* because it does place less confident players *on the spot*.) The lone sounding pitch will immediately sound sharp, flat, or in tune with the released pitch.

You may be wondering how this is so when surely the entire section was not accurately matching accurate pitch. The reason this *pitch barometer* technique works so well is because the sum of the parts equals the whole. In other words, the *whole* sound moves to the closet in-tune pitch. Allow the players to determine the relation of their pitch to the *whole*, while encouraging them to follow their first instinct. If we think too long on the direction of our pitch, then our ears can be easily confused and not know which direction to move at all. The goal is for a student to independently and instantly identify pitch relations and make immediate adjustments. Using the *Pitch Barometer* a few seconds at every rehearsal will certainly involve students more actively with their ears! ➤●

# Best Tuning Notes by Instrument

# PART 9

When tuning with an ensemble, students do not have a choice to select an individual tuning pitch and are obligated to tune to the concert pitch mandated by the director. However, based upon the acoustics and physical construction of each wind instrument, some notes are considered to be a more appropriate tuning note than others. By tuning an instrument to its individual recommended pitch (Table 9.1), the instrument is better in tune with itself and places the instrument at its most ideal acoustical length.

**Table 9.1.** Recommended Tuning Notes for each Instrument

| Instrument | Best Tuning Note for each Instrument | Comments |
|---|---|---|
| Flute | A     D | *First check that cork of headjoint is in aligned distance to center of embouchure tone hole. Then tune the headjoint draw-length by playing these two octave Ds (fingering D creates a closed tube to which the flute has been acoustically designed.) |
| Oboe | A | Most stable/satisfactory tuning note; common orchestra tuning pitch |
| Clarinet | G     C  Barrel joint  Middle joint | Tune the G with the barrel joint **before** tuning the C with the middle joint; (most bands begin tuning clarinets on their C, however, if you first tune C with the barrel, it makes the throat tones flat to the rest of the instrument.) |
| Saxophone | F♯ | Most reliable tuning note. Tune with the mouthpiece. |
| Bassoon | C     A | Most reliable tuning notes. Tune with the bocal length # or reed strength. (Never adjust by pulling out on the bocal) |
| Horn | F     C  with trigger (Bb-side)  (Tune both sides)  open 4th partial (*in tune*) | C is an open 8th partial on F horn (no trigger) and is considered an in-tune partial. C is an open 6th partial on Bb horn (with trigger), but allow it to tune slightly sharp because the 6th partial is naturally sharp. Tune with main tuning slide. |

*continues*

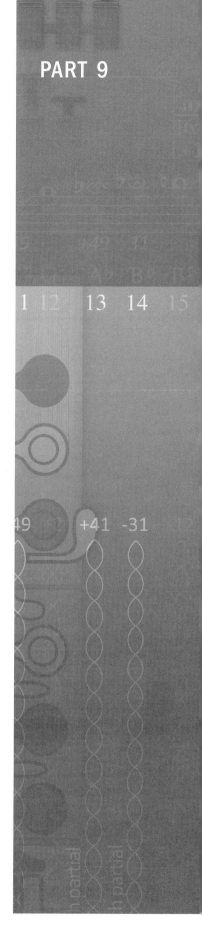

| Instrument | Best Tuning Note for each Instrument | Comments |
|---|---|---|
| Trumpet | (music notation: G, C in treble clef) | C is open, 2nd and 4th partial; considered in-tune partials in harmonic series.<br>G is open, 3rd partial, but allow it to tune slightly sharp because this is a slightly sharp partial in the harmonic series<br>Tune with main tuning slide. |
| Trombone | (music notation: B♭, F in bass clef) | Bb is 1st position, 2nd and 4th partial; considered in-tune partials in harmonic series.<br>F is 1st position, 3rd partial, but slightly lengthen slide position when tuning because this is a slightly sharp partial.<br>Tune with main tuning slide. |
| Euphonium | (music notation: B♭, F in bass clef) | Bb is open, 2nd and 4th partial; considered in-tune partials in harmonic series.<br>F is open, 3rd partial, but allow it to tune slightly sharp because this is a slightly sharp partial in the harmonic series<br>Tune with main tuning slide. |
| Tuba | (music notation: B♭, F in bass clef) | Bb is open, 2nd and 4th partial; considered in-tune partials in harmonic series.<br>F is open, 3rd partial, but allow it to tune slightly sharp because this is a slightly sharp partial in the harmonic series<br>Tune with main tuning slide. |

**Note:** Information compiled from interviews with selected professional music educators/artists.

## BEST TUNING NOTES FOR THE ENSEMBLE

It is best to tune to both Concert Bb and Concert F before a rehearsal or a performance. Concert Bb is a good tuning note for the majority of the ensemble as it works well within a practical range of the overtone series for most the instruments. Using Concert F provides the horns a better tuning pitch than Bb, and it further allows the clarinets to tune throat tone G by adjusting with the barrel joint. (Keep in mind, however, that Concert F is a terrible tuning note for saxophones.) Table 9.2 provides a suggested tuning routine that may be varied from day to day.

**Table 9.2.** 5-Minute Ensemble Tuning Routine

| | |
|---|---|
| **1 minute** | Play Concert Bb or F **Scale** in half notes & other variations (emphasize listening for ensemble tone and balance at the **Unison**) |
| **1 minute** | Play Concert Bb or F **Scale Steps**: I – III – I – V – I; I – III – V – III – I (emphasize listening for correct **interval pitch approach**)<br>Sing Concert Bb or F Scale Steps: I – III – I – V – I; I – III – V – III – I |
| **1 minute** | Play Concert Bb or F **Chords**: in scale tonic of F, Bb and Eb (eventually add entire Circle of 4ths/5ths to the routine).<br>A variation is to divide the band into groups and play a harmonized scale in canonic fashion as follows:<br>Group 1: 1 2 3 4 5 6 7 8 7 6 5 4 3 2 1 ——— (sustain tonic)<br>Group 2:      1 2 3 4 5 6 7 8 7 6 5 4 3 2 1 —— (sustain tonic)<br>Group 3:           1 2 3 4 5 6 7 8 7 6 5 4 3 2 1 — (sustain tonic)<br>Group 4:               1 2 3 4 5 6 7 8 7 6 5 4 3 2 1<br>(emphasize listening for interval pitch at the **Octave, Fifth, and Third**) |
| **45 seconds** | Play Concert Bb or F in quarter notes: **Scale Steps** 5 - 6 - 7 - 8(1) (emphasize listening for correct pitch **approach to tonic**)<br>Sing Concert Bb or F in quarter notes: **Scale Steps** 5 - 6 - 7 - 8(1) |
| **45 seconds** (15 seconds per each tuning note) | then have principal **tuning** instrument sound a Bb, F, and A for ensemble; (emphasize adjusting length of instrument to the one *best* note of the three given for your instrument instead of using other methods to bring pitch to tuning center) |

There are many opinions as to the best method of tuning a band, yet none are really incorrect if the method promotes players to hear for themselves. Our goal is to create independent players with great ears! Going up and down each row with an electronic tuner while instructing a student to push in or pull out is detrimental to developing independent aural skills. Here is one method used to tune an ensemble. (Director may choose to sound Concert F or Bb as the tuning reference.)

1.  Principal clarinetist sounds tuning reference joined by principal tuba. Both of these players use an electronic tuner. (No other member of the band is allowed to use a tuner.) (The clarinet and tuba MUST be held responsible to have their instrument warmed-up and in tune before they sound the tuning pitch.)

2.  Principal players from each section sound the tuning note and make adjustments as necessary.

3.  Repeat step 1

4.  Principal players sound the tuning note followed by the remainder of players in each section.

If an ensemble is especially large, the director may want to use the following tuning process.

1.  Principal clarinetist sounds tuning reference joined by principal tuba. Both of these players use an electronic tuner. (No other member of the band is allowed to use a tuner.) (The clarinet and tuba MUST be held responsible to have their instrument warmed-up and in tune before they sound the tuning pitch.)

2.  Principal players from each Brass section sound the tuning note and make adjustments as necessary.

3.  Repeat step 1

4.  Principal Brass players sound the tuning note followed by the remainder of players in each brass section.

5.  Repeat step 1

6.  Principal players from each Woodwind section sound the tuning note and make adjustments as necessary.

7.  Repeat step 1

8.  Principal Woodwind players sound the tuning note followed by the remainder of players in each woodwind section.

A variation of the above is to include singing as part of the regular tuning process as such:

1.  Principal clarinetist sounds tuning reference joined by principal tuba. Both of these players use an electronic tuner. (No other member of the band is allowed to use a tuner.) (The clarinet and tuba MUST be held responsible to have their instrument warmed-up and in tune before they sound the tuning pitch.)

2.  All sing Concert Bb (or Concert F)

3.  Principal players from each section sound the tuning note and make adjustments as necessary, while band is still singing

4.  Repeat step 1

5.  All sing Concert Bb (or Concert F)

6.  Principal players sound the tuning note followed by the remainder of players in each section.

Ed Lisk suggests tuning an ensemble as follows:

1.  Tuba sustains F concert, point to the principal euphonium player to sound the octave F. The volume will be less than the tuba sound. The euphonium must become a *part* of the tuba sound.

2.  When the tuba and euphonium have achieved *beatless octaves,* proceed with the 1st trombone. Tuba and euphonium will continue sounding the F concert, taking a breath when necessary.

3.  Continue this process with all remaining principal players. As each player achieves beatless sound, the next principal player above comes in and builds upon all others to that point. This process is followed all the way to the piccolo player.

4.  When all principal players have achieved beatless octaves, stop and have the tuba sound F concert again and this time have the bassoons, and contra clarinets tune to the tuba.

5.  Alto and Baritone Saxophones tune both F and Bb Concert and compensate for the sharpness of F Concert. Use the same beatless tuning procedures for Bb Concert.

6.  Once all principal players have tuned unison and octaves, start with the Tuba again playing an F concert.

7.  Principal players will follow the same process, but this time other section members will enter one at a time after their principal section leader enters.

8.  Section players use the "3 Logical Steps to Effective Balance and Blend"

    *If you hear yourself above all other, 1 of 3 things is happening:*

    i.   *You are overpowering or overblowing!* Make the necessary adjustment.

    ii.  *You are playing with poor tone quality!* Make the necessary adjustment (embouchure, breath support, posture, reed, etc.)

    iii. *You are playing out of tune!* Make the necessary adjustment by extending or shortening the length of your instrument (Lisk, 1987, p. 71–73).

Repeating the tuning note by the principal clarinetist/oboist and tuba player throughout the tuning process is important to keep the tuning note from *wandering off course* as it passes throughout each section. The author likes to use a clarinet to tune as the majority of players in the woodwind section will be clarinetists and therefore easier for them to tune off a pitch from their own instrument timbre. However, add the tuba to the initial tuning pitch because it is the lowest instrument of the band and therefore the other instruments can fit their sound into the sounding overtones of the tuba. It is best not to use an oboist to sound the initial tuning note until such time that they are able to consistently sound a full, resonant, steady pitch.

Students should be instructed to play with a full tone at a *mf*. It is also helpful to articulate the tuning note rather than simply sustaining the note. Sustaining a note often tends to "trick" the player's ears into hearing a faulty pitch in tune after sitting on it for a short while. Articulating the note with a *Daw* or *Too* can help a player hear the initial pitch of each attack. Players need to be further instructed to hear the pitch internally before sounding the pitch externally. [Refer to *Chapter Six: Tone Quality* in the book *Teaching Instrumental Music: Developing the COMPLETE Band Program* (Meredith Music Pub.) by Shelley Jagow for more detailed information on aural imaging.] Upon completing the tuning process, the ensemble should alternate singing and playing a few unison pitches. As part of the warm-up procedure, singing can help prepare the players mentally as well as physically.

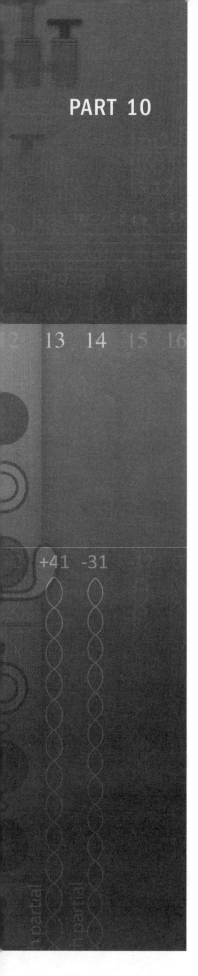

# PART 10

# Tuning Matrix by Instrument

## FLUTE

| Causes Pitch to Play FLAT | Causes Pitch to Play SHARP |
|---|---|
| Head-joint pulled out | Head-joint pushed in |
| Air stream directed down | Air stream directed up |
| Lower lip covers more embouchure plate | Lower lip covers less embouchure plate |
| Low range of flute (generally) | High range of flute (generally) |
| Dynamics decrease (softer) | Dynamics increase (louder) |
| Temperature drops (colder) | Temperature rises (warmer) |
| Slower air speed | Faster air speed |
| General Comments | |

- Flute should sound between a G—A on stopped or open head-joint alone.
- Check cork position in head-joint so that mark on cleaning/tuning rod appears in center of tone hole; 17 mm from end.
- Head-joint should **not** be pulled out more than 1/4"
- Overblow low C fingering to match tuning of the octave. Do the same with low D. This helps to put the flute in tune with itself as well as determine what pitch it was manufactured to play at—A440 or A442, etc.

\* Pitch adjustment on flute should be manipulated more with the embouchure and air direction rather than *rolling in/rolling out.*

## OBOE

| Causes Pitch to Play FLAT | Causes Pitch to Play SHARP |
|---|---|
| Reed pulled out | Reed pushed in |
| Less reed in mouth | More reed in mouth |
| Reed tip opening is too open | Reed tip opening is too closed; (this will also occur as reed ages) |
| Reed length is too long | Reed length is too short |
| Reed that is softer/easier | Reed that is harder |
| Embouchure is more relaxed | Embouchure is more firm |
| Low range of oboe (generally) | High range of oboe (generally) |
| Dynamics increase (louder) (pitch not as predictable as it is with single reeds) | Dynamics decrease (softer) (pitch not as predictable as it is with single reeds) |
| Slow unfocused air speed | Fast and pinched air speed |
| Temperature drops (colder) | Temperature rises (warmer) |
| General Comments | |

- Oboe reed alone should "crow" octave C's (concert pitch).
- Instrument should play at A=440 with the reed pushed all the way in.

## CLARINET

| Causes Pitch to Play FLAT | Causes Pitch to Play SHARP |
|---|---|
| Barrel is pulled out too much; (instrument is too long) | Barrel is pushed in too much; (instrument is too short) |
| Barrel that is longer | Barrel that is shorter |
| Reed that is too soft | Reed that is too hard; will often induce biting |
| Embouchure is too loose (too little pressure from jaw and/or corners not pulled in) | Embouchure is too firm (too much pressure from jaw and/or corners pulled in too tight/biting) |
| Lay of mouthpiece is too open | Lay of mouthpiece is too closed |
| Angle of mouthpiece entry is held too far out | Angle of mouthpiece entry is held too close in |
| Dynamics increase (louder) | Dynamics decrease (softer) |
| Slow unfocused air speed | Fast and pinched air speed |
| Temperature drops (colder) | Temperature rises (warmer) |
| General Comments | |

- Soprano Clarinet should sound around concert **C** on mouthpiece (with reed) alone.
- Bass Clarinet should sound around a concert **F#** on mouthpiece (with reed) alone.
- Standard barrel length = 66 mm.
- Standard mouthpiece is one of medium lay and medium tip opening.
- Although not highly recommended, an option to consider is using tuning rings as they may help seal the barrel for better response, keep the barrel from sliding back in after tuning, and help players maintain more consistent tuning (when conditions are consistent).

## SAXOPHONE

| Causes Pitch to Play FLAT | Causes Pitch to Play SHARP |
|---|---|
| Mouthpiece is pulled out | Mouthpiece is pushed in |
| Reed that is softer | Reed that is harder |
| Embouchure is more loose | Embouchure is more firm |
| Lay of mouthpiece is more open | Lay of mouthpiece is more closed |
| Angle of mouthpiece entry is held further out | Angle of mouthpiece entry is held closer in |
| Low range of saxophone (generally) | High range of saxophone (generally) |
| Dynamics increase (louder) | Dynamics decrease (softer) |
| Slow unfocused air speed | Fast and pinched air speed |
| Temperature drops (colder) | Temperature rises (warmer) |
| General Comments | |

- Soprano Saxophone should sound around a concert **C** on mouthpiece (with reed) alone.
- Alto Saxophone should sound around a concert **A** on mouthpiece (with reed) alone.
- Tenor Saxophone should sound around a concert **G** on mouthpiece (with reed) alone.
- Baritone Saxophone should sound around a concert **D** on mouthpiece (with reed) alone.
- Standard mouthpiece is one of medium lay and medium tip opening.

## BASSOON

| Causes Pitch to Play FLAT | Causes Pitch to Play SHARP |
|---|---|
| Bocal is longer (no. 3 or 4) | Bocal is shorter (no. 0 or 1) |
| Reed pulled out | Reed pushed in |
| Reed that is softer | Reed that is harder |
| Reed tip opening is too open | Reed tip opening is too closed |
| Reed length is too long | Reed length is too short |
| Embouchure is more relaxed | Embouchure is more firm |
|  | Lower range of bassoon (generally) |
| Dynamics increase (louder) (pitch not as predictable as it is with single reeds) | Dynamics decrease (softer) (pitch not as predictable as it is with single reeds) |
| Slow unfocused air speed | Fast and pinched air speed |
| Temperature drops (colder) | Temperature rises (warmer) |
| **General Comments** ||
| ▪ Bassoon should sound a concert pitch somewhere between Eb–A on reed crow alone. ▪ Standard bocal length = no. 2 (no. 3 on Fox models) ||

## BRASS

| Cause Pitch to Play FLAT | | | | Cause Pitch to Play SHARP | |
|---|---|---|---|---|---|
| Valve combination :    23 (slightly flat) | | | | Valve combinations:    12 (slightly sharp)    13 (sharp)    123 (very sharp) | |
| Notes in 5th and 7th partials | | | | Notes in 3rd and 6th partials | |
| Slides pulled out | | | | Slides pushed in | |
| Cup mutes | | | | Straight & Harmon mutes | |
| Cup that is deeper | | | | Cup that is more shallow | |
| Embouchure is more loose | | | | Embouchure is more firm | |
| | | | | High range (generally) | |
| Dynamics decrease (softer) | | | | Dynamics increase (louder) | |
| Temperature drops (colder) | | | | Temperature rises (warmer) | |
| Off-stage playing may sound flat, so player may want to play a bit sharp to compensate. | | | | | |
| **Valve Combination** | **Pitch Tendency** | **Semitone change** | | **Solution for pitch tendency:** | |
| 0 | in tune | 0 | 0 | | |
| 2 | in tune | 1 | 1/2 step | | |
| 1 | in tune | 2 | 1 step | | |
| 12 | slightly sharp | 3 | 1 1/2 steps | Use 1st-valve slide with 12 combination | |
| | | | | Use 3 as substitute for sharp 12 combination | |
| 23 | slightly flat | 4 | 2 steps | lip up | |
| | | | | Use 14 as substitute for flat 23 combination | |
| 13 | sharp | 5 | 2 1/2 steps | Use 3rd-valve slide with 13 combination | |
| | | | | Use 4 as substitute for sharp 13 combination | |
| 123 | very sharp | 6 | 3 step | Use 1st- and 2nd- valve slides with 123 combination | |
| | | | | Use 24 as substitute for sharp 123 combination | |
| **General Comments** ||||||
| ▪ The 1st valve lowers the fundamental by a tone, the 2nd valve by a semitone, and the 3rd valve by a tone and a half. ▪ 6% Rule: In order to lower the pitch a half-step, the length of a brass instrument must be increased by approximately 6%. ▪ The longer the valve combination, the more sharp the instrument will become. ▪ The fundamental, second, fourth and eighth partials (same note, different octaves) correspond exactly with the equal tempered scale and are therefore in-tune. ▪ A sharp fingering used on a flat partial (5th or 7th) may assist with better pitch production, but a sharp fingering used on a sharp partial (3rd or 6th) will be unbearably sharp. ||||||

# How to Tune Slides of Brass Instruments

# PART 11

**Horn**

| | | |
|---|---|---|
| **HORN – Tuning each valve slide** Version A: *(matching both sides of horn)* <br> *Recommended for Beginning Students through High School Level* <br> <u>Note</u>: Tune with *standard* right hand position in which the RH is slightly cupped, with fingers flat against the far (away from you) bell wall. | | |
| **STEP 1** <br><br> **open-valve** | Play C (on B♭-Side) <br><br> Tune this note with the **Main Slide** (with the aid of a tuner or sounding pitch.) <br><br> *[The Main Tuning Slide is found by following the lead pipe to the first tuning slide you come to.]* | ...then *match* the tuned C on Bb-side, to the open C on F-side by using the **F-Tuning slide** <br><br> If F-side is flat, push in on F-Main Slide. If F-side is sharp, pull out on F-Main Slide. |
| **STEP 2** <br><br> **2nd-valve** | Play B (on B♭-Side) <br><br> Tune this note with **Bb-2nd-valve slide** (with the aid of a tuner or sounding pitch.) | ...then *match* the tuned B on Bb-side to 2nd-valve B on F-side by using the **F-2nd-valve slide** |
| **STEP 3** <br><br> **1st-valve** | Play B♭ (on B♭-Side) <br><br> Tune this note with **Bb-1st-valve slide** (with the aid of a tuner or sounding pitch.) | ...then *match* the tuned Bb on Bb-side, to 1st-valve Bb on F-side by using the **F-1st-valve slide** |
| **STEP 4** <br><br> **3rd-valve** | Play A (on B♭-Side) <br> Tune this note with **Bb-3rd-valve slide** to be *slightly flat* (Why? a flat 3rd-valve provides a good alternative to use with sharper combinations) <br><br> [Then check the 1-2 combination; it is okay if it plays *slightly sharp*] | ...then *match* the tuned A on Bb-side, to 3rd-valve A on F-side by using the **F-3rd-valve slide** |
| *(Optional step)* <br> **STEP 5** <br><br> **2/3 combo** | Play A♭ (on B♭-Side) <br> It is okay if 2-3 is *slightly flat* (due to valve combination)* <br> <u>AND</u> <br> it is also okay if 2-3 is *slightly sharp* (due to sharp 6th partial) <br> * On some newer horn models, the 2/3 combo can actually be **sharp** | ...then *match* the tuned Ab on Bb-side, to 2-3 Ab on F-side <br> *You may need to push/pull the F-3rd-valve slide a bit to compromise.* |
| **OTHER FACTORS:** | • Brass instruments are designed to play sharp if valve slides are pushed all the way in. Thus, the slides should be pulled out a little (1/4" - 1/2") before you begin tuning. <br> • Many experts recommend to tune the Bb side of the horn before the F side; otherwise you will undo the tuning of the F side if you tune it before the Bb side. <br> • In general, on F-side the valve slides should be pulled out slightly more than Bb-side (these valves are located below/behind the F side) because the F side of horn is longer than the Bb side. | |
| **TIP:** | • If you are unsure of which slides belong to which horn, then pull out the slide and blow air through the horn. If you get a stuffy tone without the thumb trigger depressed, then the slide belongs to the F horn; if you get a stuffy tone with the thumb trigger depressed, then the slide belongs to the Bb horn. <br> • Younger students: With a pencil, mark on the valve slides where they should approximately be so the student can place the slide back in the proper position length after emptying water from that particular slide. After a while, a player will memorize how far each slide is pulled out. | |

*continues*

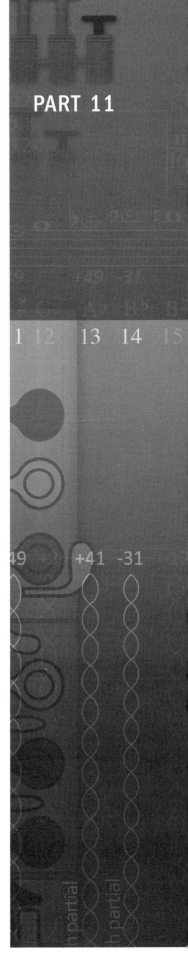

| HORN – Tuning each valve slide | | | Version B: (tuning to 4th/8th harmonic) |
|---|---|---|---|
| <u>Note:</u> Tune with *standard* right hand position in which the RH is slightly cupped, with fingers flat against the far (away from you) bell wall. | | | |
| **STEP 1**<br><br>open-valve | Play octave F's<br>on B♭-Side | Play octave C's<br>on F-Side | Tune on Bb-side with **Main Slide**<br>Tune on F-side with **F-Tuning Slide**<br><br>*This tunes both octaves to in-tune partials of 4th and 8th harmonic.* |
| **STEP 2**<br><br>2nd-valve | Play octave E's<br>on B♭-Side | Play octave B's<br>on F-Side | Tune with **2nd-valve slide**<br>(on respective sides)<br><br>*This tunes both octaves to in-tune partials of 4th and 8th harmonic.*<br><br>*[Younger players should tune only to the lower octave until embouchures are more developed.]* |
| **STEP 3**<br><br>1st-valve | Play octave E♭'s<br>on B♭-Side | Play octave B♭'s<br>on F-Side | Tune with **1st-valve slide**<br>(on respective sides)<br><br>*This tunes both octaves to in-tune partials of 4th and 8th harmonic.* |
| **STEP 4**<br><br>2/3 combo | Play octave D♭'s<br>on B♭-Side | Play octave A♭'s<br>on F-Side | Tune with **3rd-valve slide**<br>(on respective sides)<br><br>*Although tuning to in-tune partials of 4th and 8th harmonic, it is okay if the 2/3 combo is **slightly flat** due to nature of flat valve combination.* *<br><br>\* However, on some newer horn models, the 2/3 combo can actually be **sharp** |
| **OTHER FACTORS:** | • Brass instruments are designed to play sharp if valve slides are pushed all the way in. Thus, the slides should be pulled out a little (1/4" - 1/2") before you begin tuning.<br>• Many experts recommend to tune the Bb side of the horn before the F side; otherwise you will undo the tuning of the F side if you tune it before the Bb side.<br>• In general, on F-side the valve slides should be pulled out slightly more than Bb-side (these valves are located below/behind the F side) because the F side of horn is longer than the Bb side. | | |
| **TIP:** | • If you are unsure of which slides belong to which horn, then pull out the slide and blow air through the horn. If you get a stuffy tone without the thumb trigger depressed, then the slide belongs to the F horn; if you get a stuffy tone with the thumb trigger depressed, then the slide belongs to the Bb horn.<br>• Younger students: With a pencil, mark on the valve slides where they should approximately be so the student can place the slide back in the proper position length after emptying water from that particular slide. After a while, a player will memorize how far each slide is pulled out. | | |

## Trumpet

<table>
<tr><td colspan="3">Tuning the Trumpet<br>As a starting point, push the slides all the way in, and then pull out the main tuning slide 1/2"–1"</td></tr>
<tr>
<td>Play C<br>(Concert Bb)<br>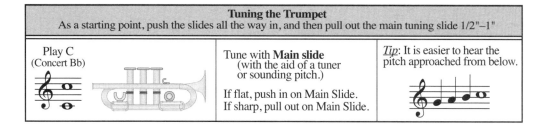</td>
<td>Tune with Main slide<br>(with the aid of a tuner<br>or sounding pitch.)<br><br>If flat, push in on Main Slide.<br>If sharp, pull out on Main Slide.</td>
<td>Tip: It is easier to hear the<br>pitch approached from below.</td>
</tr>
</table>

## Trombone

<table>
<tr><td colspan="4">Trombone F-Attachment Tuning</td></tr>
<tr><td colspan="2">• The main tuning slide should be pulled out slightly (1/2"-1") before you start to tune.</td><td colspan="2">• Depress the F-attachment trigger when moving the F-Main Slide.</td></tr>
<tr>
<td>STEP 1</td>
<td>Play Concert Bb (or Concert F for younger players)</td>
<td>Tune with main tuning slide:<br><br>If flat, push in.<br><br>If sharp, pull out.</td>
<td>…then match your tuned F to the F an octave lower with F-trigger depressed.<br>Tip: Younger players should tune only to high F until embouchure is more developed.</td>
</tr>
<tr>
<td>STEP 2</td>
<td>Play Concert F with the F-attachment<br>V1</td>
<td></td>
<td>Tip: It is easier to hear the pitch approached from below.<br>This also assists players to hear various positions in tune.</td>
</tr>
</table>

## Euphonium

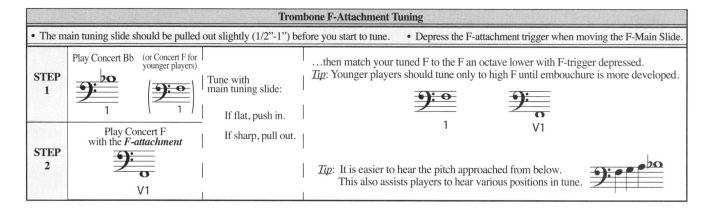

<table>
<tr><td colspan="4">Euphonium - Tuning each Slide</td></tr>
<tr><td colspan="4">As a starting point: • the main slide should be pulled out no more than 1/2",<br>• the 1st slide should be pulled out about a 1/4",<br>• the 2nd slide should be pushed in all the way,<br>• and the 3rd and 4th slide pulled out just a bit ( no more than a 1/4")</td></tr>
<tr>
<td>Play Bb</td>
<td></td>
<td>Tune with Main slide</td>
<td>open 2nd & 4th partial<br>If flat, push in on slide.<br>If sharp, pull out on slide.</td>
</tr>
<tr>
<td>Play A</td>
<td></td>
<td>Tune with 2nd slide</td>
<td>2nd & 4th partial<br>If flat, push in on slide.<br>If sharp, pull out on slide.</td>
</tr>
<tr>
<td>Play Ab</td>
<td></td>
<td>Tune with 1st slide</td>
<td>2nd & 4th partial<br>If flat, push in on slide.<br>If sharp, pull out on slide.</td>
</tr>
<tr>
<td>Play Gb</td>
<td></td>
<td>Tune with 3rd slide</td>
<td>2nd partial<br>If flat, push in on slide.<br>If sharp, pull out on slide.</td>
</tr>
<tr>
<td>Play F</td>
<td></td>
<td>Tune with 4th slide</td>
<td>2nd partial<br>If flat, push in on slide.<br>If sharp, pull out on slide.<br><br>It is recommended to tune the 4th-valve slightly flat so that the 2-4 combination is not too sharp.</td>
</tr>
</table>

## Tuba

| BBb Tuba - Tuning each Slide | | | |
|---|---|---|---|
| As a starting point: | • the 1st slide should be pulled out about a 1/4",<br>• the 2nd slide should be pushed in all the way,<br>• and the 3rd and 4th slide pulled out just a bit ( no more than a 1/4") | | |
| Play Bb | | Tune with **Main slide** | *open 2nd & 4th partial*<br>If flat, push in on slide.<br>If sharp, pull out on slide. |
| Play A | | Tune with **2nd slide** | *2nd & 4th partial*<br>If flat, push in on slide.<br>If sharp, pull out on slide. |
| Play Ab | | Tune with **1st slide** | *2nd & 4th partial*<br>If flat, push in on slide.<br>If sharp, pull out on slide. |
| Play Gb | | Tune with **3rd slide** | *4th partial*<br>If flat, push in on slide.<br>If sharp, pull out on slide. |
| Play F | | Tune with **4th slide** | *4th partial*<br>If flat, push in on slide.<br>If sharp, pull out on slide.<br><br>*It is recommended to tune the 4th-valve slightly flat so that the 2-4 combination is not too sharp.* |

# Tuning Truths

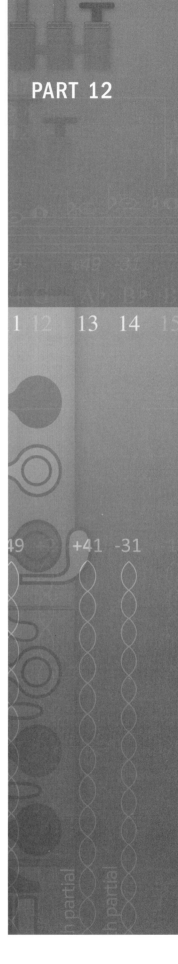

# PART 12

## PITCH DISCRIMINATION

1. Every tuning system has its own deficiencies, and every instrument has its own tuning deficiencies. Despite all the research and the most refined fingering and tuning charts that exist, nothing is superior to the EAR!

2. The further out-of-tune the pitches, the faster the resulting beats; the closer to in-tune the pitches, the slower the resulting beats.

3. Most players can discriminate pitch between tones as small as +/− 10 cents or up to 20 cents (Madsen, 1969; Parker, 1983).

4. Both professional and amateur musicians are able to discriminate flatness better than sharpness (Elliot, 1983; Karrick, 1998; Wapnick & Freeman, 1980).

5. Presence of strong overtones leads to better overall pitch perception (Cassidy, 1989; Ely, 1998; Platt and Racine (1985).

6. Tone that is brighter in timbre is perceived to be sharper in pitch (Worth, 1998).

7. Both professional and amateur musicians are able to perform an isolated pitch with greater accuracy than when performing melodic pitches (Morrison, 2000).

8. The greater the melodic complexity, the more performers are distracted from attending to the single parameter of pitch matching (Morrison, 2000).

9. Usually, but not always, a player performs sharp on descending intervals, and performs flat on ascending intervals (Duke, 1985; Yarbrough, Karrick & Morrison 1995).

10. Pitch deviation is usually greater in just intonation than it is in equal temperament (Karrick, 1998).

11. Equal-tempered tuning can be considered as *controlled mistuning* in order to force intervals to be compatible with true octaves. (Stegeman, 1967)

12. Bb does not equal the frequency of A# in any tuning system except equal tempered tuning.

13. Unisons that are played out-of-tune are often more discordant than intervals played out-of-tune because unison partials are coinciding with each other. (Stegeman, 1967)

14. An octave equivalent always produces a ratio of 2:1 whether the tuning system is just, Pythagorean, or equal temperament. (Asmussen)

15. The perfect fifth (P5) is always tuned to the ratio 3:2 whether the tuning system is just, Pythagorean, or equal temperament. (Asmussen)

## PITCH ADJUSTMENT

16. It is better to tune a bit sharp than flat because it is easier to humor a pitch down than up.

17. Both professional and amateur musicians have a tendency to err in the sharp direction more than the flat direction (Karrick, 1998; Morrison, 2000).

18. Not all instruments are tuned to A440, thus the intonation tendencies may be different for instruments tuned to different frequencies. For example, most woodwind instruments are tuned to A440, but some marked with an "H" are tuned to a higher pitch, and others marked with an "L" are tuned to a lower pitch.

19. Although not absolute, playing instruments of similar brand, model and quality will be easier to tune with each other than an array of instrument brands, models and quality.

20. The newer the model of a quality instrument the less exaggerated the typical tendencies will be.

## TEMPERATURE & DYNAMICS

21. As temperature rises, wind instruments become sharp, but string instruments (strings, harp, piano) and percussion instruments (mallet percussion, timpani) become flat. As temperature falls, wind instruments become flat, but string instruments (strings, harp, piano) and percussion instruments (mallet percussion, timpani) become sharp.

22. The longer the tubing of an instrument, the more pitch is affected by temperature changes. (Therefore a piccolo is least affected, while a tuba is most affected.)

23. Valve brass instruments are built at the factory to be sharp (at room temperature) if slides are pushed all the way in. An instrument should never be tuned with slides pushed all the way in.

24. As dynamics increase, wind instruments tend to play sharp, with the exception of single reed instruments, which tend to play flat. As dynamics decrease, wind instruments tend to play flat, with the exception of single reed instruments, which tend to play sharp.

25. A lack of breath support will cause the pitch to go flat, with the exception of single reed instruments, which tend to play sharp with a lack of breath support.

## EMBOUCHURE

26. On any wind instrument, an embouchure too tight will cause the pitch to play sharp, and an embouchure too loose will cause the pitch to play flat.

27. On all wind instruments, it is easier to flatten a pitch than it is to raise a pitch with the embouchure alone.

## VALVES & TONE-HOLES (INSTRUMENT LENGTH)

28. 4th-valve can be substituted for 1st- and 3rd-valve combination. (Using alternate fingerings will result in variations of timbre from original fingerings.)

29. 3rd-valve can be substituted for 1st- and 2nd-valve combination. (Using alternate fingerings will result in variations of timbre from original fingerings.)

30. 2nd- and 4th-valve can be substituted for 1st-, 2nd- and 3rd-valve combination. (Using alternate fingerings will result in variations of timbre from original fingerings.)

31. Although mature clarinetists tend to play sharp above high C (above staff), young clarinetists tend to play flat above high C due to an embouchure that is not yet fully developed.

32. Although mature bassoonists tend to play sharp above high G (above staff), young bassoonists tend to play flat above high G due to an embouchure that is not yet fully developed.

33. A compensating 4-valve instrument is approximately half of the pitch variance of a non-compensating 4-valve instrument. (For example, if a non-compensating pitch is typically 66-cents sharp, then the compensating pitch will be approximately 33-cents sharp.)

34. Compensating 3 and 4 valve instruments. The instrument "compensates" for the inherent sharp valve-combination of first and/or second used in combination with the third-valve, by adding additional length by means of loop-tubing. (An excellent illustration of how the compensating system works is provided by David Werden in an online flash video: http://www.dwerden.com/comp/aCompIntro6_FlowFlow_F4.html)

35. The fourth valve on euphonium and tuba compensate for the most out-of-tune notes, and provides for extended lower range (lowers the fundamental a fourth).

36. The 4th-valve on euphonium and tuba function like the F-valve on trombone in that both lower the fundamental by a fourth.

37. Young trombone players often play 2nd position too low and 6th/7th positions too high.

38. The longer the vibrating column the more difficult it is for a brass player to control the pitch. Therefore, trumpet pitch can be more greatly controlled by the player's lips than other brass instrument. Trombones can compensate by adjusting their slide, horns by adjusting their right hand position, and euphonium and tuba by using a fourth valve (if they have one). In other words, the trumpet trigger/ring mechanism is a "luxury" while the low brass fourth valve is "essential". (Stauffer, 17, 1989)

39. Valve brass instruments may use alternate fingerings in the harmonic series to assist in adjusting pitch for certain chord positions, but trombones should use regular slide positions and merely adjust length of slide. [Example: In concert Ab, a trumpet player has a fourth-line D in the staff; this note is the M3 of the chord and could be fingered 1 versus 13 to play a flat concert C, which brings it into tune.]

40. On woodwind instruments, closing keys/holes can lower a pitch, and opening keys/holes can raise a pitch. (Using alternate fingerings will result in variations of timbre from original fingerings.)

41. The clarinet has a cylindrical bore that only allows for odd-numbered partials to resonate. Although this creates a "purer" tone due to the absence of even-numbered partials, it does create greater intonation difficulties.

42. Pulling the barrel joint on the clarinet will slightly affect the overall pitch, but significantly affects the pitch of the throat tones. (The pitch of throat tone Bb is changed in pitch four times as much as its neighbor clarion tone of B). (Stauffer, 1989)

43. All wind instruments must be lengthened in order to lower the pitch, and must be shortened in order to raise the pitch.

## RANGE

44. Although mature oboists and clarinets tend to play sharp above high A (above staff), young players tend to play flat in the high register due to an embouchure that is not yet fully developed.

45. On oboe, the low register tends to be flat and the upper register tends to be sharp.

46. On clarinet, the throat tones (G, G#, A, A#) can be flarp[1]. However, most school clarinets (student models) tend to play the throat tones sharp due to the instrument's cylindrical bore. However, this pitch tendency is remedied

---

1 Although *flarp* is not yet a word distinguished by *The New Grove Dictionary of Music*, flarp may be considered slang to define a pitch tendency that can be either sharp or flat, or so out-of-tune it is difficult to tell what the pitch direction is.

in clarinets (professional model) that have a polycylindrical bore; in fact, the throat tones can sometimes be flat on some professional models.

47.  The flute, oboe and clarinet have opposite pitch tendencies of the bassoon and saxophone in their low register. (Flutes, oboes and clarinets are typically flat in the low register while bassoons and saxophones are typically sharp in the low register.)

48.  On piccolo, the middle register often tends to be sharp, while the upper register is flat.

## MUTES AND HAND

49.  A straight or Harmon mute will cause the pitch to play sharp.

50.  A cup or plunger mute will cause the pitch to play flat. With a cup mute the pitch will become flatter the higher in the register a player plays. With a plunger mute the pitch will become flatter the more the bell is covered by the plunger.

51.  On horn, the pitch will play sharp if the player's hand is not far enough in the bell, or flat if the player's hand is too far into the bell.

52.  On muted horn or partially stopped horn, the pitch will play flat.

53.  On fully stopped horn, the pitch will play a half-step sharp, and therefore players must use fingerings a half-step below the written pitch (Boldin, 2008). [Play stopped horn on the F side regardless of the register. If stopped horn is played on the Bb side then the pitch will play 3/4 tone sharp. However, in the higher register it may be better to use fingerings on the Bb side. Choose the fingering that provides the best tone and pitch accuracy.] [Since all hand sizes and shapes are different, and since there are several different bell shapes and sizes, every person must experiment on his or her own to find the best stopped sound and intonation, even if it means using unconventional fingering.]

## HARMONICS

54.  Young trombonists often play 2nd and 3rd positions too long (thus flat), and 5th, 6th, and 7th positions too short (thus sharp).

55.  Cymbals, unlike wind instruments, will sound more than one fundamental and thus have several overtones ringing.

56.  On brass instruments, the 5th harmonic is flat and the 6th partial is sharp.

57.  Any two notes played simultaneously will produce a third note called a *resultant tone.* The frequency of the resultant tone is the difference of the two frequencies being played. (Leuba, 1980; Hindemith, 1945)

58.  Partials 1, 2, 4 and 8 will always have the same pitch name in any given overtone series.

59. Players on valve brass instruments can sometimes use various *partial-fingerings* to improve tuning, but trombone players, with the aid of their ear, should only use *regular-positions* and make minor length adjustments on the slide.

60. Some intervals have varying ratios. Directors thus have a choice in determining which interval size to use. Typically, it is recommended to use the smaller intervals for minor keys and larger intervals for major keys.

61. Choose fingerings wisely. Make knowledgeable decisions based on priority of facility, timbre or pitch. Typically we select a fingering that performs with best pitch and timbre for slower passages, and choose a fingering that performs with best technical facility for faster passages.

## MOUTHPIECES & REEDS

62. Most intonation issues on the oboe and bassoon are a result of a poor reed. Buy quality reeds preferably made by a respected area oboist/bassoonist versus a generic store-bought reed.

63. Double reed players can raise pitch by taking in more reed, or lower pitch by taking in less reed.

64. Clarinet and saxophone mouthpieces that have a lay/facing too close will tend to play sharp, while a lay that is too open will tend to play flat.

65. Mouthpieces with a small chamber tend to play sharper than those with a larger chamber.

66. Mouthpieces with a shallow baffle tend to play sharper than those with a deeper baffle.

67. Metal mouthpieces will play sharper than plastic mouthpieces, and plastic mouthpieces tend to play sharper than rod-rubber mouthpieces.

68. Brass players on a mouthpiece with a very shallow cup tend to play sharp. (Ely, 2009)

69. Small-bore mouthpieces tend to play sharper than large-bore mouthpieces.

**Figure 12.1.** Clarinet and Saxophone Mouthpiece Design

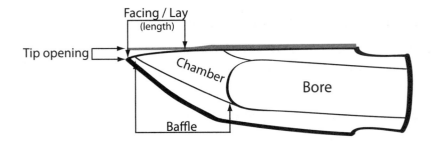

## TUNING SYSTEMS

70. It is best to use equal temperament tuning versus just tuning when performing atonal music. (Papich and Rainbow, 1974)

71. It is best to use equal-tempered tuning or Pythagorean tuning for linear tuning (melodic), and use just tuning for vertical tuning (harmonic).

**Figure 12.2.**

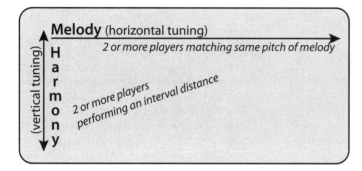

72. Just tuning is not a perfect system for a piece with several modulations

# Bibliography

Asmussen, Robert. *A Rule-based System for Tuning Chord Progressions.* Accessed: http://www.terraworld.net/c-jasmussen/tunex/rules.htm#Rules%20Detailed%20Heuristics

Bain, Peter. *Physics of Music: An optional course given to first year physics students.* Accessed: http://www-users.york.ac.uk/~pm1/PMweb/Physics_of_Music_notes.pdf

Bain, Reginald (2003). *The Harmonic Series: A Path to understanding musical intervals, scales, tuning and timbre.* Paper published online at University of South Carolina School of Music. Accessed December 21, 2011 at http://www.music.sc.edu/fs/bain/atmi02/

Barbour, J. Murray (1967). *Tuning and Temperament: A Historical Survey.* East Lansing: Michigan State College Press.

Blackwood, Easley (1985). *The Structure of Recognizable Diatonic Tunings.* New Jersey: Princeton University Press.

Boldin, James (2008). *Horn: stopped and muted.* The Instrumentalist, September, 48–51.

Brasch, Harold (1997). *The Euphonium and Four Valve Brasses.* (Reprint of original 1971 edition); TUBA Press

Campbell, Murray and Clive Greated (1987). *The Musician's Guide to Acoustics.* New York: Schirmer, pp. 84–86 and 165–167.

Cassidy, J. W. (1989). The effect of instrument type, stimulus timbre, and stimulus octave placement on tuning accuracy. *Missouri Journal of Research in Music Education, 26,* 7–23.

Coy, Benjamin. Proper placement of the minor seventh in untempered (just) intonation. Accessed June 7, 2011: http://www.tenorposaune.com/music/minor7.pdf.

Doty, David B. (2010). *The Just Intonation Primer.* (3rd ed.) www.dbdoty.com/Words/Primer1.html

Duke, R. A. (1985). Wind instrumentalists intonation performance of selected musical intervals. *Journal of Research in Music Education, 33*(2), 101–111.

Elliot, C. A. (1983). Range distribution, timbre, and cent calibration as factors in pitch discrimination capacities. Bulletin of the Council for Research in Music Education, no. 75, 59–62.

Ely, Mark C. (1988). The effects of timbre on intonational performance and perception by collegiate performers of selected woodwind instruments (Doctoral dissertation, Ohio State University). *Dissertation Abstracts International, 49*(9), 2442A. (University Microfilms No. AAT 8824494).

Ely, Mark and Amy Deuren (2009). *Wind Talk for Woodwinds. A Practical Guide to Understanding and Teaching Woodwind Instruments.* New York, NY: Oxford University Press.

Ely, Mark and Amy Deuren (2009). *Wind Talk for Brass: A Practical Guide to Understanding and Teaching Brass.* New York, NY: Oxford University Press.

Farkas, Phillip (1956). *The Art of French Horn Playing.* Seacaucus, NJ: Summy-Birchard Music.

Garofalo, Robert (1996). *Improving Intonation in Band and Orchestra Performance.* Ft. Lauderdale, FL: Meredith Music Publications.

Gingras, Michele (2006). *Clarinet Secrets—52 Performance Strategies for the Advanced Clarinetist.* Scarecrow Press, Inc.: Lanham, MD.

Gingras, Michele (2011). *More Clarinet Secrets: 100 Quick Tips for the Advanced Clarinetist.* Scarecrow Press, Inc.: Lanham, MD.

Goldman, Richard. F. (1961). *The Wind Band.* Boston, MA: Allyn and Bacon, Inc.

Haynes, Bruce (2002). *A History of Performing Pitch.* MD: Scarecrow Press, Inc.

Helmholtz, Hermann (1954). *On the Sensations of Tone.* New York, NY: Dover Publications.

Hindemith, Paul (1945). *Craft of Musical Composition.* Associated Music Publishers, New York. Vol. 1, p. 57.

Jagow, Shelley (2007). *Teaching Instrumental Music: Developing the COMPLETE Band Program.* Galesville, MD: Meredith Music Publications.

Johnston, Ben (2006). *Maximum Clarity and Other Writings on Music.* Chicago, IL: University of Illinois Press

Karrick, Brant (1998). *An Examination of the Intonation Tendencies of Wind Instrumentalists Based on Their Performance of Selected Harmonic Musical Intervals.* Journal of Research in Music Education 46, no. 1, 112–127, Spring 1998.

Kent, Earle L. (1956). *The Inside Story of Brass Instruments.* Elkhart, IN: C. G. Conn Ltd.

Leenman, Tracy (2008). *Understanding your musical instruments.* School Band and Orchestra, September, 20–26.

Lehman, Arthur (1980). *The Art of Euphonium Playing.* Poughkeepsie, NY: Robert Hoe.

Leuba, Christopher (1984). *A Study of Musical Intonation.* Prospect Publications.

Lisk, E. S. (1987). *The Creative Director: Alternative Rehearsal Techniques* (3rd ed.). Ft. Lauderdale, FL: Meredith Music.

Lisk, E. S. (1996). *The Creative Director: Intangibles of Musical Performance.* Ft. Lauderdale, FL: Meredith Music.

Madsen, C. K., Edmonson III, F. A., & Madsen, C. H. (1969). *Modulated frequency discrimination in relationship to age and musical training.* Journal of the Acoustical Society of America, 46, 1468–1472.

Meyer, Max F. (1929). *The Musician's Arithmetic.* Boston, MA: Oliver Ditson Company.

Middleton, James, Harry Haines, and Gary Garner (1998). *The Band Director's Companion.* San Antonio, TX: Southern Music Company.

Morris, Gareth (1991). *Flute Technique.* New York, NY: Oxford University Press.

Morrison, Steven J. (2000). *Effect of Melodic Context, Tuning Behaviors, and Experience on the Intonation Accuracy of Wind Players.* Journal of Research in Music Education 48, no. 1, 39–51, Spring 2000.

Neubäcker, Peter (1993). *What does 'just intonation' mean?* Harmonik & Glasperlenspiel. Beiträge.

Norwood, Leah (2005). *Horn Harmonics Wheel.* Villa Grande, CA: Horn Harmonics Enterprises. www.hornharmonics.com

Papich, George and Edward Rainbow (1974). *A pilot study of performance practices of twentieth-century musicians.* Journal of Research in Music Education 22, 31.

Parker, O. (1983). Quantitative differences in frequency perceptions by violinists, pianists, and trombonists. Bulletin of the Council for Research in Music Education, no. 76, 49–58.

Phillips, Harvey and William Winkle. (1992). *The Art of Tuba and Euphonium.* Seacaucus, NJ: Summy-Birchard Music.

Pizer, R. A. (1976). *How to Improve the High School Band Sound.* West Nyack, NY: Parker Publishing Co.

Polansksy, Larry, Daniel Rockmore, Micah K. Johnson, Doublas Repetto, and Wei Pan (2009). *A Mathematical Model for Optimal Tuning Systems.* Perspectives of New Music, 47/1:69–110, Winter, 2009.

Pottle, Ralph R, and Mark H. Hindsley. (1970). *Tuning the School Band and Orchestra.* Hammond, LA: C. G. Conn.

Renold, Maria (2004). *Intervals, scales, tones and the concert pitch.* Forest Row: Temple Lodge.

Ridenour, Thomas W. (2000). *Clarinet Fingerings: A Comprehensive Guide for the Performer and Educator.* Duncanville, TX: W. Thomas Ridenour.

Ridenour, Thomas W. (2000). *The Educator's Guide to the Clarinet.* Denton, TX: W. Thomas Ridenour.

Rider, Wendell (2006). *Real World Horn Playing.* San Jose, CA: W. Rider Publications.

Roberts, C. (1975). *Elements of Brass Intonation.* The Instrumentalist, March, 86–90.

Smith, C. M. (2004). *Why all the "Mystery"?* School Band and Orchestra, August 2004, 18–21.

Snow, Donald B. (2006). *A Conductor's Guide to Wind Instrument Deficiencies.* Dissertation: The University of Southern Mississippi.

Stauffer, Donald (1989). Intonation Deficiencies of Wind Instrument. Stauffer Press: Birmingham, AL.

Stegeman, William (1967). *The Art of Music Intonation.* The Instrumentalist, May-October Issues.

Van Tongeren, Mark C. (2004). *Overtone Singing. Physics and Metaphysics of Harmonics in East and West.* (Revised second edition), Amsterdam, The Netherlands: Fusica.

Wapnick, J., & Freeman, P. (1980). *Effects of dark-bright timbral variation on the perception of flatness and sharpness.* Journal of Research in Music Education, 28, 176–184.

Worthy, M. D. (1998). Effects of tone quality conditions on perception and performance of pitch among selected wind instrumentalist. *Dissertation Abstracts International,* 59(2). 442A. (University Microfilms No. AAT 9825134).

Yarbrough, C., & Ballard, D. (1990). The effect of accidentals, scale degrees, direction, and performer opinions on intonation. Update: Applications Research in Music Education (Spring-Summer), 19–22.

Yarbrough, C. Karrick, B., & Morrison, S. J. (1995). Effect of knowledge of directional mistunings on the tuning accuracy of beginning and intermediate wind players. *Journal of Research in Music Education,* 43(3), 232–241.

# Artist Consultation

## FLUTE

Katherine **Borst Jones**; Professor, Ohio State University (Columbus, OH)

Bonita **Boyd**; Flute Professor, Eastman School of Music (Rochester, NY)

Dr. Philip **Dikeman**; Associate Professor, Blair School of Music at Vanderbilt University (Nashville, TN)

Dr. Brian A. **Luce**; Associate Professor, The University of Arizona (Tucson, AZ); Yamaha Performing Artist

Dr. Rochelle **Mann**; Professor, Music Education and Department Chair at Fort Lewis College (Durango, CO).

Paula **Robison**; Donna Hieken Flute Chair at New England Conservatory (Boston, MA); Soloist and Recording Artist

Dr. Laurel **Zucker**; Professor, California State University (Sacramento, CA); Conn-Selmer Artist and Recording Artist/Composer with Cantilena Records/Publications

## OBOE

Katherine **DeGruchy**; Oboe Professor, Wright State University (Dayton, OH)

Kristin R. **Reynolds**, Oboe Professor, Eastern Michigan University (Ypsilanti, MI), English Horn with the Toledo Symphony Orchestra

Dr. Martin **Schuring**; Professor, Arizona State University (Tempe, AZ)

## CLARINET

Dr. Christopher **Ayer**: Professor, Stephen F. Austin School of Music (Nacogdoches, TX)

James **Campbell**; Professor, Indiana University Jacobs School of Music (Bloomington, IN); Recording Artist, Conn-Selmer Artist Clinician

Dr. Michele **Gingras**; Distinguished Professor, Miami University (Oxford, OH); Rico Artist Clinician and Buffet Crampon Artist Clinician

Kenneth **Grant**; Associate Professor, Eastman School of Music (Rochester, NY)

John **Kurokawa**; Clarinet Professor, Wright State University (Dayton, OH); Principal Clarinet Dayton Philharmonic Orchestra and Cincinnati Chamber Orchestra; Yamaha Performing Artist

Dr. Lynn A. **Musco**; Professor, Stetson University School of Music (DeLand, FL); Buffet Group USA Artist-Clinician

## SAXOPHONE

Dr. Susan **Fancher**; Saxophone Professor, Duke University (Durham, NC); Conn-Selmer Artist-Clinician and Vandoren Performing Artist

Dr. Jonathan **Helton**, Professor, University of Florida (Gainesville, FL); Conn-Selmer Artist-Clinician

Dr. Shelley **Jagow**; Professor, Wright State University (Dayton, OH); Conn-Selmer Artist-Clinician and Rico Artist-Clinician; Meredith Music and Hal Leonard Clinician

Dr. Otis **Murphy**; Professor, Indiana University Jacobs School of Music (Bloomington, IN); Yamaha Artist-Clinician and Vandoren Performing Artist

Dr. Timothy **Rosenberg**; Saxophone Artist and Course Director at Full Sail University (Winter Park, FL)

Dr. William **Street**; Professor, University of Alberta (Edmonton, AB, Canada); Conn-Selmer Artist-Clinician

Dr. Kenneth **Tse**; Professor, University of Iowa (Iowa City, IA); Yamaha Performing Artist

## BASSOON

Rodney **Ackmann**; Assistant Professor, University of Oklahoma (Norman, OK)

Bill **Jobert**; Bassoon Professor, Wright State University (Dayton, OH)

Dr. Scott **Pool**; Assistant Professor, The University of Texas at Arlington (Arlington, TX)

## TRUMPET

Edmund **Cord**; Professor, Indiana University Jacobs School of Music (Bloomington, IN); Former Principal Trumpet Israel Philharmonic Orchestra, Utah Symphony, Santa Fe Opera

Keith **Johnson**; Professor, The University of North Texas (Denton, TX)

Dr. Christopher **Moore**; Professor, Florida State University (Tallahassee, FL)

Dr. Marc **Reed**; Director of Brass Studies and Professor at Fort Lewis College (Durango, CO); Conn-Selmer Artist-Clinician and Co-Principal Trumpet with San Juan Symphony Orchestra

Dr. Karl **Sievers**; Professor, University of Oklahoma (Norman, OK); Principal Trumpet of the Oklahoma City Philharmonic and the University of Oklahoma Brass Quintet; Conn-Selmer Artist-Clinician

Dr. Mark **Wilcox**; Associate Professor, McMurry University (Abilene, TX)

Dr. Daniel **Zehringer**; Assistant Professor, Wright State University (Dayton, OH); Principal Trumpet with Springfield Symphony Orchestra and Cincinnati Ballet Orchestra

## HORN

Dr. Richard **Chenoweth**; Professor, University of Dayton; Graul Chair in Arts & Languages, (Dayton, OH)

Dale **Clevenger**; Grammy Award Winner; Principal Horn Chicago Symphony Orchestra since February 1966 (Chicago, IL).

Daniel **Katzen**; Associate Professor of Horn at the University of Arizona School of Music; former member of Boston Symphony Orchestra.

Peter **Kurau**; Principal Horn Rochester Philharmonic; Professor of Horn at the Eastman School of Music (Rochester, NY).

Jonas **Thoms**, Horn Professor, Wright State University (Dayton, OH)

Sean **Vore;** Freelance Horn Artist; Assistant Principal Horn in the Dayton Philharmonic Orchestra (Dayton, OH)

Terrisa **Ziek**, Professor of Horn at Emporia State University (KS); C.G. Conn Horn Artist

## TROMBONE

Gretchen **McNamara**; Trombone Professor, Wright State University (Dayton, OH)

Sam **Saltar**; Trombone Solo Concert Artist and Conn-Selmer Artist; former member of Philadelphia Philharmonic Orchestra

Deb **Scott**; Associate Professor of Trombone at Stephen F. Austin State University (Nacogdoches, TX)

## EUPHONIUM

Adam **Frey**; Yamaha Euphonium Performing Artist and Instructor of Euphonium at Georgia State University (Atlanta, GA).

Jason **Ham**; Yamaha Performing Artist and Euphonium with the U.S. Army West Point Band (West Point, NY).

Francis H. **Laws**, Emeritus Faculty at Wright State University; Principal Euphonium/Soloist with Ohio Valley British Brass Band, Colorado Brass Band, and Great Western Rocky Mountain Brass Band.

Brian **Meixner**, Assistant Professor, High Point University (High Point, NC)

## TUBA

Adam **Frey**; Yamaha Euphonium Performing Artist and Instructor of Euphonium at Georgia State University (Atlanta, GA).

Dr. Yutaka **Kono;** Assistant Professor; Director of Orchestra at The University of Vermont (Burlington, VT).

Dr. Benjamin **Miles**; Associate Professor; Middle Tennessee State University (Murfreesboro, TN).

Dr. Benjamin **Pierce**; Professor; The University of Arkansas (Fayetteville, AR)

## THEORIST

Dr. William **Alves**; Professor; Harvey Mudd College (Claremont, CA).

Dr. Franklin **Cox**; Associate Professor; Wright State University (Dayton, OH).

Dr. Dean **Drummond**; Professor; Montclair State University (Montclair, NJ)

Dr. Kyle **Gann**; Associate Professor; Bard College (Annandale-on-Hudson, NY).

Dr. Michael **Harrison**; Composer and Pianist; Just Intonation Theorist (New York, NY).

Dr. David **Hykes**; Theorist; David Hykes and the Foundation Présence Harmonique (France).

Dr. Larry **Polansky**; Professor; Dartmouth College (Hanover, NH).

# Glossary

**Balance** occurs when two or more tones combine with one another to achieve a *complementary* sound.

**Beat**, in acoustics, is when two sounds interfere with one another due to each pitch vibrating at a slightly different frequency. The slower the beats sound the closer they are to matching pitch; and the faster the beats sound the further away they are from matching pitch. A beat-less sound indicates that the two tones are vibrating at the same frequency.

**Blend** occurs when two or more tones combine with one another to achieve a *unity* of sound.

**Cent** is a unit of measurement for an interval based on frequency ratios. A cent is 1/1200 of an octave. An equal-tempered semitone is equal to 100 cents.

**Consonance** (coinciding partials) is created not only by the interval created by the fundamental tones, but also by the quantity of aligned partials created by each fundamental.

**Dissonance** (conflicting partials) is produced by the quantity of semitone and whole-tone partial conflicts created by the fundamental tones.

**Equal-Temperament** is a tuning system in which the adjustment or *tempering* of intervals have equal width (semitone =100 cents). Equal tempered instruments such as a piano makes it simple to modulate and play in any key.

**Intonation** is the action of playing/singing in tune. Intonation may be flat, sharp, or in tune.

**Flarp** is not a word distinguished by any dictionary—yet, but may be considered slang to define an intonation that can be sharp, flat or so out-of-tune that it is difficult to tell the actual pitch direction.

**Frequency** is the number of occurrences per unit of time that a cycle is repeated. When the unit of measurement is in seconds, the frequency is the hertz (Hz). Hz = number of cycles per second. Musical instruments produce varying frequencies that qualify its range and produce specific notes.

**Fundamental** is the lowest frequency of a waveform and thus the primary (fundamental) note of the harmonic series. The fundamental is also defined as the first partial.

**Just Temperament** is a tuning system in which the adjustment or *tempering* of intervals is based on harmonic ratios. Just tempered instruments make it difficult to modulate and play in more than one key.

**Harmonics**: see Overtones

**Overtones** are the pitches sounded as multiple frequencies above the fundamental. The fundamental in combination with the corresponding overtones creates the harmonic series. The first overtone is also defined as the second partial above the fundamental first partial.

**Pitch** is a quality of sound that may be definite (a fixed position in a scale) or indefinite (sound produced by cymbal). Pitch is determined by the fundamental produced by the frequencies of the harmonic series. The pitch of a tone is determined by the rate of speed of vibrations (called the *frequency*), which is measured in cycles per second.

**Pythagorean Temperament** is a tuning system in which the adjustment or *tempering* of intervals is based on the ratio 3:2 or the perfect fifth. Pythagorean tuning creates a wolf fifth (smaller than a just perfect fifth) which makes it difficult to modulate and play in more than one key.

**Resonance** is measured by the quality of amplitude when the pitch of an instrument vibrates at the same frequency to the natural harmonic series.

**Semitone** is a unit of tonal measurement for the smallest interval. An equal tempered semitone is equal to 1/12 of an octave, which equals to 100 cents and is referred to as a minor 2nd. In just intonation there are two different sizes of semitones: 1) major (diatonic) semitone with a ratio 16:15 is equal to 112 cents, and 2) a minor (chromatic) semitone with a ratio of 17:16 is equal to 105 cents.

**Timbre** is the characteristic sound or tone color of an instrument. Variations in timbre are created by quality of resonance.

**Tone** is an interval equal to the sum of two semitones. An equal-tempered whole tone is equal to 200 cents and is referred to as a Major 2nd. In just intonation there are two different sizes of whole tones: 1) Major tone with a ratio 9:8 is equal to 204 cents, and 2) a minor tone with a ratio of 10:9 is equal to 182 cents.

# About the Author

**Dr. Shelley Jagow** is Professor of Music at Wright State University (Dayton, OH) where she serves as director of the Symphonic Band and Saxophone Quartet. She earned top honors in Music Education degrees from the University of Saskatchewan (Canada) and the University of Missouri (Columbia) where respective mentors include Marvin Eckroth, Dale Lonis, Martin Bergee and Wendy Sims. She earned her Ph. D. in Music Education at the Union Institute & University (Cincinnati) where Colonel Timothy Foley, Frank Battisti, and Edward Wingard served as her mentors. In addition to studies in education, saxophone and conducting, Shelley also earned the Certificate in Piano Performance IX from the Royal Conservatory of Music (Toronto, Canada).

In 2009 Shelley was nominated for the "Robert J. Kegerreis Distinguished Professor of Teaching" Award. As artist clinician with Conn-Selmer, Hal Leonard, JW Pepper and Rico, "Dr. J" enjoys working with high school bands and presents clinics, performances, adjudications, and serves as honor band conductor at various state, national and international conferences and events. Venues include locations in Alberta, California, Connecticut, Japan, Florida, Kansas, Illinois, Indiana, Italy, Manitoba, Massachusetts, Nebraska, New Hampshire, New York, Ohio, Ontario, Oregon, Rhode Island, Saskatchewan, South Carolina, Texas, Utah, Virginia and Washington D.C. Some of the activities include the MENC (Music Educators National Conference), the Midwest International Band and Orchestra Clinic, NASA (North American Saxophone Alliance), ISME (International Society for Music Education), CMS (College Music Symposium), and the United States Navy Band International Saxophone Symposium. Shelley coaches the WSU student *Avion Saxophone Quartet*, which can be heard on CDbaby.com. Shelley can be heard performing on the Emeritus Recording label, on National Public Radio Performance Today, and America's Millennium Tribute to ADOLPHE SAX, Volume XI by Arizona University Recordings.

Shelley has published numerous articles in periodicals such as the *College Music Symposium Journal*, *TRIAD*, *Music Educators Journal*, *National Association of College Wind and Percussion Instructors*, *Canadian Winds*, and *Canadian Band Journal*. She is a regular contributing author to the *Teaching Music Through Performance in Band* series (GIA Music), and *The Music Director's Cookbook* (Meredith Music Publications). Shelley is the author of the book and DVD *Teaching Instrumental Music: Developing the Complete Band Program* (Meredith Music Publications), a resource rapidly becoming the adopted textbook for music education degree study across the United States and Canada. She recently completed archiving over thirteen hours of historical music lectures by legendary saxophonist Jean-Marie Londeix (and translated by William Street, University of Alberta) released in 2012 on a multi-dvd set *The Londeix Lectures*; available on FaceBook.com and AdolpheSax.com by searching Londeix Lecture DVD.

Contact information:   Email: shelley.jagow@wright.edu
                Website: www.wright.edu/~shelley.jagow/

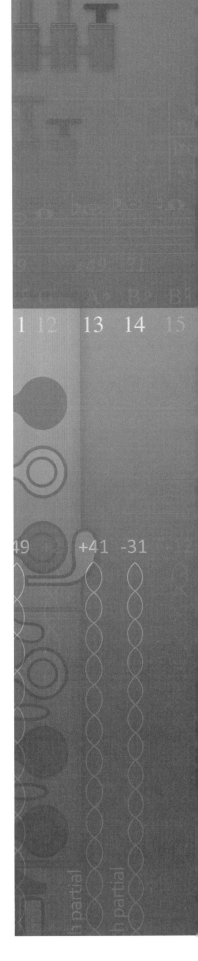

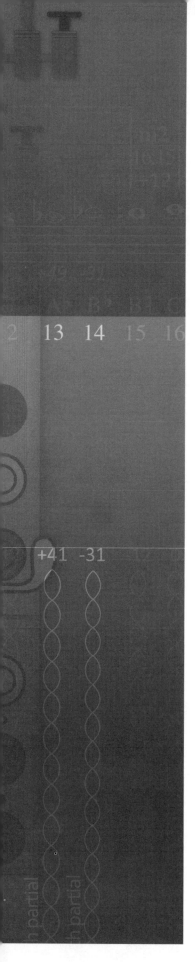

# Index